PRAYER WARRIOR
M♥M

PRAYER WARRIOR MOM

*Covering your kids
with God's blessings and protection*

Marla Alupoaicei

THOMAS NELSON
Since 1798

NASHVILLE   DALLAS   MEXICO CITY   RIO DE JANEIRO

Published in Nashville, Tennessee, by Thomas Nelson. Thomas Nelson is a registered trademark of Thomas Nelson, Inc.

Published in association with Books & Such Literary Agency, Mary Keeley, 5926 Sunhawk Drive, Santa Rosa, California 95409-5370, www.booksandsuch.biz.

Image in chapter 3 used by permission. *Live a Praying Life* by Jennifer Kennedy Dean, New Hope Publishers, newhopedigital.com.

Thomas Nelson, Inc., titles may be purchased in bulk for educational, business, fund-raising, or sales promotional use. For information, please e-mail SpecialMarkets@ThomasNelson.com.

Unless otherwise noted, Scripture quotations are taken from THE NEW KING JAMES VERSION. © 1982 by Thomas Nelson, Inc. Used by permission. All rights reserved.

Scripture quotations marked AMP are from THE AMPLIFIED BIBLE: OLD TESTAMENT. © 1962, 1964 by Zondervan (used by permission); and from THE AMPLIFIED BIBLE: NEW TESTAMENT. © 1958 by the Lockman Foundation (used by permission).

Scripture quotations marked GW are from GOD'S WORD Translation. Copyright © 1995 by God's Word to the Nations. Used by permission of Baker Publishing Group.

Scripture quotations marked NASB are from NEW AMERICAN STANDARD BIBLE®. © The Lockman Foundation 1960, 1962, 1963, 1968, 1971, 1972, 1973, 1975, 1977, 1995. Used by permission.

Scripture quotations marked NIV are taken from the Holy Bible, New International Version®, NIV®. Copyright © 1973, 1978, 1984, 2011 by Biblica, Inc.™ Used by permission of Zondervan. All rights reserved worldwide. www.zondervan.com

Scripture quotations marked NIV 1984 are from the Holy Bible, New International Version®, NIV®. Copyright © 1973, 1978, 1984 by Biblica, Inc.™ Used by permission of Zondervan. All rights reserved worldwide. www.zondervan.com

Scripture quotations marked NLT are taken from the Holy Bible. New Living Translation copyright © 1996, 2004, 2007 by Tyndale House Foundation. Used by permission of *Tyndale House Publishers Inc.*, Carol Stream, Illinois 60188. All rights reserved.

Library of Congress Cataloging-in-Publication Data

Alupoaicei, Marla, 1974–
  Prayer warrior mom : covering your kids with God's blessings and protection / Marla Alupoaicei.
    p. cm.
  Includes bibliographical references (p.   ).
  ISBN 978-1-4002-0435-9
1. Mothers—Religious life. 2. Intercessory prayer—Christianity. I. Title.
  BV4529.18.A55 2013
  242'.6431—dc23   2012025603

Printed in the United States of America

13 14 15 16 17 RRD 6 5 4 3 2 1

*To Dorothy Martin, my faithfully devoted
Prayer Warrior Mom—your love and prayers
have transformed my life. Thank you!*

*To my darling husband, David, I love you more than you
know. Your love makes every place a magical place.*

*And to my children, Evan and Eden, you are my priceless
treasure and the sunshine of my life. I will always love you.*

*"Prayers are the winged messengers
to carry the need to God."*
—JOHN W. FOLLETTE, *BROKEN BREAD*

Contents

Contents

Introduction

A BOOK IS ONLY AS GOOD AS IT IS TIMELY," SAYS MY friend Carol.

And my cool writers-group friend, Ben, says, "The right book at the right time is like God performing a mini-miracle in your life."

Here's to your mini-miracle, Prayer Warrior Mom!

This is your year, my friend. Your year of spiritual breakthrough. Your year of jubilee. Your year to live as a victor rather than a victim. Your year to see your children start loving God and living for Him. Your year to rejoice as your lost lamb returns to the fold. Your year to "lay aside every weight, and the sin which so easily ensnares . . . [and] run with endurance the race that is set before [you]" (Heb. 12:1–2).

You are precious and prayed for. You've been in my heart and on my mind with every word I've written. I pray that this book meets you where you are and carries you into the realm of God's infinite possibilities for you and your children. I want to see you break through to blessings that exceed your wildest dreams as you see God do "immeasurably more than all we ask or imagine, according to his power that is at work within us" (Eph. 3:20 NIV).

My Christ-anchored hope is that you'll find this book to be both timely and transformational in every aspect of your life: spiritual, mental, emotional, physical, intellectual, theological, and so much more. I believe these fifteen chapters will inspire you to establish a new habit of praying for your children with power, authority, gratitude, and renewed faith.

Would you consider starting a "Prayer Warrior Mom" group at your church and reading through this book in a semester-long or summer-long Bible study? Whether at church or in your home, I hope you'll establish a small group of praying friends that will continue to meet faithfully together as you intercede for your children. Please let me know about your Prayer Warrior Mom group (and the results of your prayers) at my website: www.PrayerWarriorMom.com.

During the writing of *Prayer Warrior Mom*, I prayed for the Lord to reveal to me some theme passages to serve as the foundation of this book. First, He led me to the following passage—profound words from the lips of Jesus as He fulfilled a centuries-old prophecy recorded in the book of Isaiah. I believe this passage also encompasses the ministry of this book:

> The Spirit of the LORD is upon Me,
> Because He has anointed Me
> To preach the gospel to the poor;

> He has sent Me to heal the brokenhearted,
> To proclaim liberty to the captives
> And recovery of sight to the blind,
> To set at liberty those who are oppressed;
> To proclaim the acceptable year of the LORD.
> (Luke 4:18–19)

The message of *Prayer Warrior Mom* aligns with Jesus' mission: to preach the gospel, to help heal the brokenhearted, to proclaim liberty to moms wounded by sin, to restore joy to your oppressed spirit, and to proclaim this year as your season of breakthrough prayer and intercession for your kids.

The second passage affirms our ministry of motherhood and reflects what our attitude should be as we serve our husbands and children "as to the Lord" (Col. 3:23). This passage undergirds everything we say and do as Prayer Warrior Moms:

> Do all things without complaining and disputing, that you may become blameless and harmless, children of God without fault in the midst of a crooked and perverse generation, among whom you shine as lights in the world, holding fast the word of life, so that I may rejoice in the day of Christ that I have not run in vain or labored in vain. (Phil. 2:14–16)

God also led me to a third passage that outlines our spiritual mission, our "marching orders" as Prayer Warrior Moms:

For though we walk in the flesh, we do not war according to the flesh, for the weapons of our warfare are not of the flesh, but divinely powerful for the destruction of fortresses. We are destroying speculations and every lofty thing raised up against the knowledge of God, and we are taking every thought captive to the obedience of Christ. (2 Cor. 10:5 NASB)

Thank you for fighting the good fight with me, for keeping the faith as we fall to our knees to do battle for our children. If you're hurting, I pray that the principles, stories, and scriptures in this book will refresh your spirit and speed your healing. May the Lord grant you "beauty for ashes" and a "garment of praise" in exchange for your heavy burden (Isa. 61:3).

In each chapter I've included model prayers, small-group discussion questions, and a crucial "Sword of the Spirit" section with Bible verses for you to read, meditate on, and memorize. All these will guide you in your quest to cover your children with prayer.

You're on your way to becoming a mighty PWM (Prayer Warrior Mom)! Your prayers for your children are already creating awe-inspiring results in the heavenly realm, as God promised in Isaiah 55:11:

My word . . . shall not return to Me void,
But it shall accomplish what I please,
And it shall prosper in the thing for which I sent it.

With love, gratitude, and prayers for you,

MARLA ALUPOAICEI

Cultivate an Attitude of Gratitude

*Feeling gratitude and not expressing it is like
wrapping a present and not giving it.*

–WILLIAM ARTHUR WARD[1]

I WAS FREE! MY HUSBAND HAD AGREED TO WATCH THE kids for a bit so I could spend a rare couple of hours at my local Christian bookstore. I swung through the Starbucks drive-thru and grabbed a skinny latte on my way over.

As I entered the store, an inscription on a beautiful Spanish-style painted tile caught my eye:

BEING A MOTHER IS A HOLY PRIVILEGE.

That truth seared my heart like a bolt of lightning. Wow! Being a mother is a *holy privilege*? Not a daily drudge? Not a joyless responsibility? Not simply what we do after leaving our "real careers" behind?

Yes, motherhood is a holy privilege. God has instituted it, ordained it, and blessed it. In fact, in some ways, the mother-child relationship is our primary earthly relationship, even more central to the core of our being than marriage. (Of course, I had to buy the plaque. I needed that daily reminder of the infinite value that God places on motherhood!)

God has gifted us with a lofty vocation, a glorious calling, and a high honor. I know that the days spent with fussy babies may seem interminably long, but the years are so short. One mom of a toddler made me laugh as she described the often-thankless tasks of motherhood. She wrote:

Having a baby is really hard. I know everyone tells you that. Everyone is right . . .

When you work on a team, and you have a boss and projects and deadlines, when you get to the end of something, someone says, "Good job." Or, "Thank you." Or, "Wow, that was smart and helpful." But Henry [my son] never looks up at me when I'm changing his diaper and says, "Good move with the wipes, Mom. Very thorough." He doesn't look up at me when I'm trying to get him to go back to sleep in the night and whisper, "Fabulous technique with the shushing and rocking. You're a genius."

It doesn't matter to Henry one little bit that I can speak French or explicate sentences or cook really good roasted salmon. What matters is that I can be there with him as long as he needs me . . . I can play with Froggie, his favorite toy, one more time, one more time, one more time.[2]

Like those endless cycles we spend playing with Henry and Froggie, each time we pray, our spiritual influence on our kids gathers momentum. We grow stronger and more confident. Our faith blossoms as we and our children begin to receive an increased outpouring of God's blessings. Our daily prayers collect with an aggregate effect, culminating in a powerful legacy of intercession. Like a warm blanket, our petitions cover our kids with God's grace and protection.

I'm thrilled that you've picked up this book. I know the Lord will bless your desire to become a Prayer Warrior Mom. I look forward to helping you engage in stronghold-shattering, breakthrough prayer for your kids.

As you begin to practice the principles, memorize the scriptures, and pray the prayers included in this book, you'll see how quickly God's truth will transform your children's hearts. At the back of this book, in the "Recommended Resources" section, I've also provided at least three additional resources on each topic I address in *Prayer Warrior Mom*. I trust they'll be inspiring and helpful to you in your journey toward becoming a victorious prayer warrior.

Most important, my fervent hope is that you'll discover that God-honoring prayer is not about rules and regulations; it's about developing a life-giving relationship with the Lord of the universe.

The Life-Giving Power of Gratitude

Cultivating a heart of gratitude is central to your role as a Prayer Warrior Mom. As you become more thankful and effective in prayer, God will transform your family life and your marriage from the inside out. You'll be amazed by the difference in your kids' hearts, attitudes, and actions as you learn to "stand in the gap" for them (see Ezekiel 22:30). You will break through to blessing as your prayers on earth engage the limitless power of your Father in heaven.

For me, having a joyful, thankful spirit used to be so easy. God created me as an optimist by nature, with a "glass half-full" perspective on life. (My husband, David, says that he's a "realist." More on that later!)

Then I had kids. Two kids, fourteen months apart, to be exact. And having children somehow broke my half-full glass and spilled out much of my joy. Sleep deprivation combined with the burden of caring for my little ones caused my once-cheerful personality to deflate until I hardly recognized myself anymore.

My son, Evan, entered the world as a preemie, weighing only three pounds. If you've ever had a preemie, you know the significance of the "2-5-8-11-2-5-8-11" schedule. Those were the times when I had to feed and change my baby every day and every night—no exceptions. If I wanted to sleep, exercise, cook, take a walk outside, or carve out some desperately needed "me time," too bad—I had to take care of the baby. On the rare occasions that Evan happened to be blessedly asleep at 2, 5, 8, or 11 o'clock, too bad—I had to wake him up.

Then, when Evan was only five months old, surprise! I

discovered I was pregnant again. I should have been thrilled, right? Instead, I could have filled a moon crater with my tears. David and I were still staggering under the responsibilities of caring for our preemie. How could we possibly take care of another baby? But I gave birth to a sweet daughter, Eden, nine months later.

Now I'm amazed that I actually thought life with one baby was difficult! In the years since my kids' births, the physical, spiritual, and emotional strain of caring for *two babies* while also trying to maintain a godly marriage, a somewhat-clean house, a ministry, and a writing career have felt like a thousand-ton millstone around my neck. (I didn't realize it at first, but I also struggled with postpartum depression.) Maybe you've been there too.

One day, after the birth of my daughter, as I passed the swimming pool, I spied a drowned butterfly floating listlessly on the surface. *That's me*, I thought, as a profound sense of grief welled up in my soul. *That's exactly how I feel.* I reached out and scooped up the butterfly's lifeless body, admiring its stained-glass wings as I gently deposited it in the grass.

A vise of despair clamped tightly around my heart. I mourned for a fallen world that robs winged creatures of the joy of flight. And I mourned for the woman I used to be. Before having children, I had felt lighthearted and exuberant, as if soaring on gossamer wings. But afterward, I had lost my spark, my zest for life. I felt leaden and lifeless, impossibly stuck in the mud of terra firma. *What's wrong with me, God?* I wondered.

It seemed that as soon as I finished one task, my husband and children placed more demands on me, or the kids had created new disasters that needed attention. I never felt I "had it all together." We moms live with this constant tension, and it can lead to simmering feelings of frustration and discontentment.

Slowly, God helped me regain my sense of joy as I relearned how to be grateful and find new ways to express my love for the Father, Son, and Holy Spirit. I had to learn to act on my faith rather than on my feelings. I discovered that gratitude is central to our worship of God, as well as to the development and nurturing of healthy human relationships.

I'm not talking about "Pollyanna praise" here. I'm talking about letting God shape, soften, and mold our hearts until we can accept everything He gives (whether it seems heavenly or horrible) and truthfully say, "The Lord gives and the Lord takes away. Blessed be the name of the Lord" (Job 1:21, paraphrased).

Gratitude is the antidote for despair and festering unhappiness. As we honor God with our praise and create "thankful moments" with our kids, we become models of redemption for them. We show them that God can remold something broken and fallen into something sacred, redeemed, and beautiful in His sight.

If you're married, your husband is the *head* of the home, but you are the *heart* of the home. Your attitudes and actions set the tone for your family. Are you grateful, spiritually focused, positive, and encouraging? Or are you ungrateful, negative, nagging, and nitpicky? When you pray, is thankfulness your first priority, or do you just tack on a few hasty words of gratitude at the end, right before the "amen"?

Some of you are single moms. If that describes you, guess

what? You're both the head and the heart of your home. I watched my mother serve her family as a single mom with five children; I know how overwhelming it can be at times. Your kids look to you as their example of gratitude; you are their model of how to live the Christian life. When you choose to live in victory, giving praise to God for everything that you do have (rather than focusing on what you don't have), you model the attitude of Christ to your kids.

Thankfulness reflects God's kingdom order; it unlocks the heavenly storehouse of His treasures. When we forget to thank Him, we miss out on many of the blessings He has prepared for us.

Now, here's the kicker: *An attitude of thankfulness does not just happen to us; we must learn to intentionally cultivate it.*

Gratitude is not just a great personality trait that certain "happy" women possess; it's a skill, a choice, and a spiritual discipline. Thankfulness lifts the shadow of despair from our darkest days. And when others look at us, if they see thankfulness even in tough times, they will also see Christ in us, the hope of glory.

As a Prayer Warrior Mom, you serve as the thermostat of your household. When you purposefully choose to start being thankful, you will immediately warm up the atmosphere of your home. God will begin to thaw the hearts of your husband and children and infuse them with joy. Your gratitude will bring forth the fruit of the Spirit: love, joy, peace, patience, kindness, goodness, faithfulness, gentleness, and self-control (Gal. 5:22–23 NASB).

The Bible tells us to "give thanks in all circumstances; for this is God's will for you in Christ Jesus" (1 Thess 5:18 NIV).

You may be thinking, *You have no idea what I'm going through. How am I supposed to give thanks in all circumstances?* You may be grieving over your prodigal child, wondering if he or she will ever return to a healthy, godly lifestyle. Maybe you're feeling devastated by a recent divorce, a job loss, financial struggles, the death of a child, a cancer diagnosis, or a family member's illness. All these can cause us to doubt God's goodness and erase our feelings of gratitude toward Him.

You and I may struggle to be thankful *for* all circumstances, but we can still be grateful *in* all circumstances. Why? Because "we know that in all things *God works* for the good of those who love him, . . . [and are] called according to his purpose" (Rom. 8:28 NIV; emphasis added). Not all situations are necessarily good, but God is good, and He causes all things to work together according to His perfect plan. We may not necessarily *feel* happy about a certain situation, but we can still express gratitude based on what we know to be true about God.

Just like gardeners, we're called to keep careful watch over our children and step in with the pruning shears when we see signs of danger. These might include:

- the "insects" of anger, withdrawal, dishonesty, bitterness, envy, and quarreling
- the "weeds" of friends who may exert a negative influence on them
- the "disease" of words, behaviors, choices, and heart attitudes that are not pleasing to the Lord

You are the first line of defense for your kids. Your prayers create an umbrella of protection over them, shielding them from spiritual, physical, and emotional harm. As you read through this book, you will learn to engage in spiritual warfare and help your children defeat "joy stealers" so they may continue to thrive in Christ.

I recently saw a wall hanging that said, "Thanksgiving is once a year. Thanks Living is all year long!" I'm sure you know a "Thanks Living" woman. She radiates joy and thankfulness. Everyone loves to be around her. She has a servant heart, a smile, and an uplifting word for everyone. She exhibits boundless energy and offers a spiritual perspective that transforms even the darkest situations.

Guess what? *You* can be that woman! How? Start infusing your prayers with adoration and thankfulness. I like to bookend my prayers with thanksgiving at the beginning and the end. According to Jesus' examples of prayer in Scripture, we should give praise to the Father before we launch into our laundry lists of personal requests.

How do we start our journey as Prayer Warrior Moms? To begin, I recommend that you purchase two inexpensive notebooks or journals. I like to use a steno notebook for my prayer requests; I record the requests on the left side and the answers on the right side. If you enjoy crafting, you can personalize the cover of your Prayer Warrior Mom notebook with pretty scrapbook paper, ribbons, and other decorations.

I bought a beautiful red-and-white journal with the words *God is Love* on the front. I use it as my "gratitude journal." I keep it separate from my prayer journal and use it to record the things for which I'm thankful.

Leave your gratitude journal in an easy-to-access place.

Every day, take a few minutes to jot down three to five things for which you're grateful. Throughout the day, whenever you think of additional blessings, write them down. Develop this into a spiritual discipline by taking a few minutes each morning or evening to record what God has done for you. Ask for accountability from your Prayer Warrior Mom group or from a trusted friend.

Every evening, during dinner or before bed, ask your kids: "What are you thankful for today? What was the high point of your day? What was the low point?" These questions provide a way for you to tap into what's happening in your children's lives on a daily basis. Allow your kids to discuss both the wonderful and the hurtful things that may have happened to them. By doing so, you will cultivate openness in your home. You may want to record your kids' responses in a separate prayer notebook or gratitude journal, as well.

Here are some practical tips to help you create an atmosphere of gratitude in your home:

- Buy several inexpensive magnifying glasses, one for you and one for each child. (I bought ours from Dollar Tree!) Take a nature walk with your kids and collect beautiful "found objects" from nature. When you get home, examine them and talk with your children about the beauty of God's creation.
- Collect magazines and help your kids cut out pictures of things they like and things they are thankful for. Use these to create a "gratitude collage" on a piece of poster board or construction paper. You can frame these or hang them in your

kids' rooms. You can also display magazine photos on a French memo board.

- Engage your children in the practice of writing thank-you notes and cards to their friends, teachers, and relatives.

- Have your kids draw or paint pictures of what they are thankful for.

- Write a letter to each of your kids, telling them specifically why you are grateful for them and how God has gifted them.

- For your husband's birthday, your anniversary, or Valentine's Day, give him a journal in which you have recorded why you are thankful for him.

- Post a gratitude chart on the wall and have your kids write down daily blessings they are thankful for.

- During your nightly prayer time, ask your kids to thank God for three new things each day. Inspire them to be creative!

As a Prayer Warrior Mom, inspire your kids to be grateful. Teach them to give all the credit to Jesus for the good things in their lives. Model thankfulness and uplift them with genuine words of honor and encouragement. Be authentic, creative, specific, and generous with your praise. Pray for your kids every day by name. Your most awesome "gardening tool" is the ability to pray Scripture for your kids. God's Word has the ultimate authority over everything in heaven and on earth. It is "alive and active" and "sharper than any double-edged sword" (Heb. 4:12 NIV).

If you have young children, take them by the hand and

lead them in prayer daily. Help them use simple words to thank God for the good things in their lives. Catch them doing things right, and say yes whenever possible. Be their coach and their cheering squad, always spurring them on to greater confidence and maturity in the faith.

Gratitude represents one of the few gifts that we can give back to God. Our words of thankfulness resound with glory in the throne room of heaven. Our Father is pleased with our praise. He basks in glory when we give Him thanks. When you and I choose to praise the Lord, He will be fully present in our hearts, in our homes, and with our children.

Today's Prayer

Heavenly Father, I love You. Thank You for being my magnificent, almighty, loving Creator God. I lift up my children [state their names here] to You today. Please help each of them to become grateful people. Forgive me (and them) for any sins of ingratitude, discontentment, or negativity. Create in us clean hearts, and give us all an attitude of thanksgiving. Thank You for Your blessings. All of our lives belong to You. Every breath we take is a gift from You. Thank You for adoring my children, Lord. Thank You for crafting them so beautifully and for numbering each hair on their heads.

Lord, help me to show appreciation and model a heart of gratitude to my husband and children each day. Keep me from taking them for granted. Teach me to be thankful to You in all circumstances, no matter how challenging. Thank You for sending Your Son, Jesus, to die in my place and to give me the gift of eternal life with You. I pray that each of my children will establish a saving relationship with You through Jesus. I praise You for all the good gifts You have given me. Help me to trust You and give glory to You in all circumstances. In Jesus' name, amen.

The Sword of the Spirit

Do not be anxious about anything, but in every situation, by prayer and petition, with thanksgiving, present your requests to God. (Phil. 4:6 NIV)

Give thanks in all circumstances; for this is God's will for you in Christ Jesus. (1 Thess. 5:18 NIV)

Therefore, since we are receiving a kingdom that cannot be shaken, let us be thankful, and so worship God acceptably with reverence and awe. (Heb. 12:28 NIV)

Through Jesus, therefore, let us continually offer to God a sacrifice of praise—the fruit of lips that openly profess his name. (Heb. 13:15 NIV)

But you are a chosen people, a royal priesthood, a holy nation, God's special possession, that you may declare the praises of him who called you out of darkness into his wonderful light. (1 Peter 2:9 NIV)

Small Group Discussion Questions

1. Do you tend to have a "glass half-full" perspective on life or a "glass half-empty" one? Why? How does this influence your ability to maintain an attitude of gratitude?

2. Who is the most grateful person you know? How does he or she model gratitude? What have you learned about thankfulness from him or her?

3. How can you incorporate more thankfulness into your prayer life and your interactions with your husband and children? Do you have a gratitude journal? If not, purchase a special notebook or journal to use only for recording your thankful moments and God's blessings.

4. What is the most recent blessing God granted to you? Did you express your gratitude to Him? If so, how? If not, take time to do so now. Think of a tangible reminder you could display or create to help commemorate God's awe-inspiring work in your life.

2

Pray Scripture

*His Word in my mouth is a powerful weapon
that gives victory in the day of conflict.*

—JOHN QUIGLEY[1]

REBECCA[*] WAS LEARNING TO MEMORIZE AND PRAY SCRIPTURE. One day, she had stopped her car at a red light when a man wearing a ski mask yanked open the passenger door. He jumped into the car, held a gun to Rebecca's head, and said, "Drive!"

Rebecca began to pray silently, begging the Lord to protect her. She had been memorizing Psalm 91:4, which says, "He will cover you with his feathers, and under his wings you

---

[*] Not her real name.

will find refuge" (NIV). She tried to remember the passage, but in her terror, she could only call to mind one word of it.

Flustered, she blurted out, "Feathers, feathers, feathers!"

The man stared at her. "Lady, you're crazy!" he exclaimed, as he flung open the car door and disappeared down the street.

God's Word works in surprising ways! Every day, as you mine the Scriptures for treasures, He will instill His truth in your mind and inscribe it on the tablet of your heart. As you pray His living, active, and powerful Word into the lives of your kids, God will use it to protect you and your family against the enemy's destructive strategies.

Praying Scripture may sound intimidating, but it's actually quite simple and rewarding. There's no right or wrong way to do it, and you'll grow more confident with practice. Begin by choosing a scripture from the "Sword of the Spirit" section at the end of this chapter. Then make it your own by incorporating each phrase of the passage into your prayers. Add your children's *names*, as well as specific details about their personal needs, struggles, and spiritual walk. You can do this by adding pronouns such as *he*, *she*, *him*, *his*, and *her* to personalize the Scripture.

Let's say that you want to pray the following verse from the end of this chapter:

> Your word is a lamp to my feet
> And a light to my path. (Ps. 119:105)

If I were praying this passage, I might say, "Lord, thank You for providing Your Word to give us light and direction. I praise You because You do not want me and my children to walk in darkness. I am grateful for Your Word that shines a light to illuminate the way for us. Please keep my children on the straight and narrow path of Your will. Help them know and love Your Word, the Bible. Always keep them walking in Your light, and keep Satan from misleading them. In Jesus' name, amen."

Pray about who your kids are now, and pray about the men and women you want them to become. Ask God to help them grow into godly adults. Pray for God to magnify their strengths and protect them from temptation as He matures them in their areas of weakness. If one or more of your children have strayed from following the Lord, claim the promises in God's Word to bring health, healing, wholeness, wisdom, and salvation in your child's life.

An excellent way to bless your children through prayer is by finding scriptures that pertain to their names, personality traits, gifts, and character qualities (both the qualities they already have and those you'd like for them to develop). Names are important to God, so they should be important to us.

Find out the meaning of your children's names and then use those insights when you pray for your kids. Buy a name book or do some online research to discover not only the literal meanings and language origins, but the spiritual meanings and connotations of your kids' names. Look up your own name too; you may be surprised at what you find! Knowing your own name's meaning and being confident in your spiritual identity will strengthen your prayer life.

One of the best name books I've found is *The Name Book* by Dorothy Astoria. Ms. Astoria lists the language/cultural origins of more than ten thousand names, along with their inherent meanings and spiritual connotations. She also provides a relevant scripture passage for each name. For my son's name, Evan, this book lists the origin as Irish, the inherent meaning as "Young Warrior," and the spiritual meaning as "Noble Protector." The scripture passage given is Philippians 4:13: "I can do all things through Christ who strengthens me."

Let's say that your teenage daughter, Zoe, is struggling with making good decisions, and you are concerned about her relationships and her reputation. You could pray, "Lord, You say in Proverbs 22 that a good name is to be more desired than great wealth, and favor is better than silver and gold. I pray for you to give my daughter, Zoe, a good name and great favor with You and others. Her name means 'life,' Father, and I pray that her life will be full of joy and pleasing to You. Keep Zoe from making decisions that would harm her heart, body, mind, spirit, or reputation. Help her to gain favor in everything she does, everywhere she goes. Help her to see herself as You do, as beautiful and perfectly loved. In Jesus' name, amen."

Another way to pray Scripture is to connect with other women who enjoy memorizing and praying God's Word. If you're new to the prayer scene or if you are still investigating what Christianity is all about, find some mature women in the faith who have more experience with this type of prayer. You'll learn from their example!

Write out your favorite scriptures on index cards, and personalize them with your children's names. Carry them in your pocket or purse, and look at them and pray over them throughout the day. You may also want to write out these special Scripture promises and give them to your children to carry with them or display in their rooms. This is a tangible reminder that you are praying for them. For example, the name Sarah means "princess." You could write, "Sarah, you are God's beautiful princess. He loves you, and He delights in you. I am praying for you to walk with Jesus every day. I am praying for God to bless and protect you, to give you wisdom and grace in all situations. Trust in Him for everything. Love, Mom."

Read different translations of the verses you are meditating on and memorizing. You can do this by gathering a few different Bibles in various translations, or by using an online resource such as Bible Gateway. Simply type in www .biblegateway.com, and you can search for any word, phrase, name, verse, or passage in the entire Bible. In addition, you can choose any translation you prefer, from a list of dozens. Each translation presents nuances of meaning and theological insights that will illuminate the Scriptures for you.

In addition, gather a few Bible study resources for yourself. You can use a Bible dictionary or concordance to look up word meanings. Then you can turn to a Bible commentary to explain the meaning of Scripture verses and passages. For this book, I used Greek and Hebrew language tools, as well as *The Strongest Strong's Exhaustive Concordance*. These concordances are available in various Bible translations and utilize a simple numeric system that lets you find and read the Greek and Hebrew meanings of words for yourself.

Knowing and praying God's Word are central to your role as a Prayer Warrior Mom. In Ephesians 6, God calls us to equip ourselves with the full armor of God. Most of the armor is for our protection and defense: *our primary "offensive weapon" is the authoritative Word of God, the Bible!* If you and I don't memorize and claim the Scriptures, we'll always be on the defense in the battle against Satan and our culture. With God's Word in our hearts, we can serve as "minesweepers" for our kids by going ahead of them and clearing the path of spiritual and physical obstacles.

Jesus himself battled Satan using the sword of the Spirit, God's memorized Word.

Satan challenged Jesus with several temptations in the wilderness. "If You are the Son of God," he taunted, "command that these stones become bread" (Matt. 4:3).

Jesus responded, "It is written, 'Man shall not live by bread alone, but by every word that proceeds from the mouth of God'" (v. 4). Jesus had fasted for forty days in the wilderness. His desire for bread must have been fierce. But He drove home the point that God's Word should be more precious and central to our lives even than our daily food.

In fact, John 1:1 introduces Jesus Himself as "the Word." He gives us salvation, inspiration, life, and light. The Greek term for *Word*, *logos*, depicts Jesus as the one who reveals the Father and fully expresses the Godhead.

Jesus came into the world to redeem God's beloved creation. He became "God with skin on." He lived out God's truth; that's why Scripture calls Him the "incarnate" Word (John 1:14 AMP). He not only fulfilled Scripture but became the culmination of all revelation (Heb. 1:1–2). Through Him, the love of God the Father flowed into the world as Jesus took on human flesh. This Incarnation represents one of the greatest spiritual mysteries of all time: the only begotten Son became Immanuel—"God with us" (Isa. 7:14; Matt. 1:23).

When we choose to trust in *every word* that God speaks, and when we implant His Word deep within our spirits, we equip ourselves to win every battle that Satan wages. Never forget that Satan is actively seeking to invade and capture the hearts, souls, and spirits of your children. First Peter 5:8 says, "Be of sober spirit, be on the alert. Your adversary, the devil, prowls around like a roaring lion, seeking someone to devour" (NASB).

God promises us in Jeremiah 29:11 that He has a magnificent plan for our children's lives; it is a good, amazing, redemptive plan. But did you realize that Satan has a plan for our kids too? His plan is terrible and destructive. He wants to destroy God's people, no matter what it takes. And he knows that if he can mislead and harm our kids, he can cripple us with worry, stress, fear, guilt, shame, and bitterness.

The book *Prayers for Prodigals: 90 Days of Praying for Your Child* by James Banks contains some of the most compelling Scripture prayers I've ever read. If you have a prodigal son or daughter, I believe you'll find great comfort from prayers such as the one that follows, based on 2 Thessalonians 2:16–17: "May our Lord Jesus Christ himself and God our Father, who loved us and by his grace gave us *eternal encouragement and good hope*, encourage your hearts and strengthen you in every good deed and word" (NIV, emphasis added).

The author wrote:

> "Eternal encouragement *and* good hope."
> I really need both right now.
> Not just for me, but for my child.
> He is far from you and needs to come home . . .
> Help me to pray, Lord Jesus . . . *Teach* me to pray . . .
> Fill me with your Spirit and let your love flow through me into my child's life.

Like the widow who "kept coming" to the judge's door until her request was answered (Luke 18:3), help me to persevere in praying "day and night" (Luke 18:7) so that I will see real progress in my child's heart.

Jesus, you said that "everything is possible for him who believes" (Mark 9:23).

"I do believe; help me overcome my unbelief!" (Mark 9:24).

Save my son, Lord! I thank you in advance for what you will do to rescue him from the "dominion of darkness" and bring him into your "kingdom of light" . . . (Col. 1:12–13).[2]

This poignant prayer from the heart of a hurting parent illustrates the astounding power of Scripture to heal our hearts and redirect our prodigals toward home.

One Prayer Warrior Mom has described some of the ways we can use Scripture memorization and prayer to thwart Satan's plans to destroy our kids. She wrote:

Discipline your mind and your tongue. Memorize at least one Scripture a week, and teach it to your children. Make regular deposits of Scriptures into your heart and mind, and the Holy Spirit will be able to make withdrawals for you when you need them the most.

Take a stand and make your declaration of faith: By the stripes of Jesus I am healed. No weapon formed against me shall prosper. Satan, you can't have my children. They belong to God, and I claim them for the kingdom of God. I have the mind of Christ, and I bring every thought captive to the obedience of Christ . . . Satan, I break your strongholds over my family. I give up all my rebellion and all my sin, and I submit myself to the lordship of Jesus Christ.[3]

When you actively pray Scripture for your children, you lay the spiritual groundwork that engages God and His holy angels to work in your children's favor. Bathe your children in Scripture prayer, and Satan will have to get lost. The Bible says, "Submit to God. Resist the devil and he will flee from you" (James 4:7).

Today's Prayer

Dear Lord, thank You for showing me that Your Word gives me victory over Satan and all the evil works of the enemy. I claim the power of Your Word to guide, protect, fill, and restore me and my children. Teach my children to love Your principles and Your commands. Help them recognize that Your truth was given for our joy, our good, and our protection.

Lord, please reveal to me the passages You want me to use to pray for my children. Give me wisdom about using the meanings of my kids' names in prayer. Guide me and give me insight as I become more confident in praying Your Word. Illuminate the Scriptures for me. Help me to personalize them for myself and my kids. I believe with confident faith that You will grant breakthroughs to me and my children as Your living and active Word tears down Satan's strongholds in our lives. Lord, I will not let Satan have my children. They belong to You. I believe You have prepared a place for them in heaven with You. Please continue to bless them as I pray Your Word over them. Infuse our family with Your love, joy, peace, and unity. In Jesus' name, amen.

The Sword of the Spirit

Your word is a lamp to my feet
And a light to my path. (Ps. 119:105)

> So shall My word be that goes forth from My mouth;
> It shall not return to Me void,
> But it shall accomplish what I please,
> And it shall prosper in the thing for which I sent it.
> (Isa. 55:11)

For the word of God is living and powerful, and sharper than any two-edged sword, piercing even to the division of soul and spirit, and of joints and marrow, and is a discerner of the thoughts and intents of the heart. (Heb. 4:12)

By faith we understand that the worlds were framed by the word of God, so that the things which are seen were not made of things which are visible. (Heb. 11:3)

> The grass withers,
> And its flower falls away,
> But the word of the LORD endures forever.
> (1 Peter 1:24–25)

Small Group Discussion Questions

1. What kind of experience do you have with praying Scripture? After reading this chapter, which methods of praying God's Word do you think will work best for you? List some ways you can start praying Scripture for your children this week.

2. Look up your children's names using either websites or a name book. What meanings did you find? What spiritual insights did you gain by discovering the meanings of your kids' names? Do these meanings seem to fit your kids' gifts and personalities? Why or why not?

3. Look up your own name. What did you find? Do you feel that your name and its meanings fit you? What spiritual significance does your name have? How does this influence your role as a Prayer Warrior Mom?

4. As the Incarnate Word, Jesus is the author of your faith—the author of your life story. How does this affect your perspective on your life and your calling as a mother? How do you think your story (and those of your children) will unfold over the next few years?

3

Stand in the Gap

Storm the throne of grace and persevere
therein, and mercy will come down.

—JOHN WESLEY

A FEW SUMMERS AGO, MY HUSBAND, DAVID, SPENT SEV-
eral days in London on his way to Romania. (He's originally
from Romania; he and I met there in 2008 while working for
an orphan ministry. You never know when or where God
might introduce you to your soul mate!) During David's time
in the UK, he bought me a variety of fun souvenirs, as well as
plenty of European chocolate. I love that man!

One of my gifts was a cute, fitted T-shirt emblazoned
with the popular logo "Mind the Gap." On the London sub-
ways, this announcement warns passengers to be careful

while crossing the gap between the train door and the station platform. "Mind the gap" is not a bad slogan for us as Prayer Warrior Moms, either!

Before the fall of man, prayer wasn't necessary. Adam and Eve enjoyed perfect communion with God and each other in the garden of Eden. But once sin occurred, it introduced a gap into the equation, creating a breach between humankind and God. That gap still exists, and we can't cross it on our own. But we can rejoice because Jesus chose to "mind the gap" for us. He willingly sacrificed His life for us on the cross. His death and resurrection built a bridge of salvation across the chasm of sin that previously separated us from our heavenly Father. When Jesus "minded the gap" for us, He reconciled us (sinful people) to a holy God.

Now, as Prayer Warrior Moms, we have the joy of standing in the gap for our children by powerfully interceding for them before our Father in heaven.

In several cases in Scripture, God looked down upon His people's sin and searched for an intercessor—a man or woman who could see the situation with spiritual eyes. He sought someone who would "storm the throne of God," grasping the seriousness of the sin problem. He called for a prayer warrior who would fall on his or her knees to ask God to act, to move, to save, to forgive, and to reconcile the breach in the system.

The prophet Ezekiel recorded the words of the Lord: "I sought for a man among them who would make a wall, and *stand in the gap* before Me on behalf of the land, that I should not destroy it; but I found no one" (Ezek. 22:30; emphasis added). And Psalm 106:23 says, "Therefore [God] said that He would destroy them, had not Moses His chosen one *stood before Him in the breach* [the gap], to turn away His wrath, lest He destroy them" (emphasis added).

Today, God is still seeking prayer warriors to stand in the gap on behalf of His beloved children. He says, "I am looking for a woman among you who will stand in the gap before Me on behalf of her children, so that Satan will not destroy them, but so that I can bless, cover, preserve, protect, and provide for them." I'm so thankful that you have chosen to step up and be that courageous and faithful woman!

In her excellent book, *Live a Praying Life*, Jennifer Kennedy Dean provides a helpful model that illustrates how God chooses to work when we "stand in the gap" for our kids.

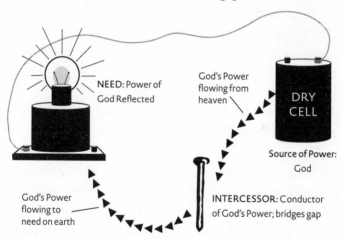

Used by permission. *Live a Praying Life* by Jennifer Kennedy Dean, New Hope Publishers, newhopedigital.com

In this illustration, the dry cell represents the power of God, ready and waiting to be released. The lightbulb represents the need on earth.

God's love for us creates a circuit in which His power and our need are connected. He is the one who pursues us; we did not pursue Him. Romans 3:11 says, "There is no one who seeks God" (NIV). Think of our lives on earth as a chess game in which God has already made the first move. His power has always been flowing toward our needs. We do not have to do anything to get this flow started. His love, resources, mercy, and provision are already moving in our direction.

Because of sin, however, the power flow reaches a gap between heaven and earth. A conductor (that's you, Prayer Warrior Mom, the intercessor!) is required for God's power to be channeled through the gap. An electric current will not jump over the air; it requires a conductor (represented by the metal nail in the diagram).

When we stand in the gap through prayer, we become the conductor of God's power and will from heaven, and we connect it to the circumstances on earth. We complete the circuit.[1]

When you and I choose to stand in the gap for our children, we reach up and pull down the blessings that God has prepared for them. First Corinthians 2:9 says, "Eye has not seen and ear has not heard . . . all that God has prepared for those who love Him" (NASB). Ephesians 2:10 says, "We are his workmanship, created in Christ Jesus for good works, which God prepared beforehand so that we would walk in them" (NASB).

Picture the rich blessings piled high and overflowing in heaven for you and your kids. I like to imagine a huge treasure chest reserved in heaven for each of my kids. One has the name Evan inscribed on it, and the other bears the name Eden. Through prayer, my husband and I have the power to open these treasure chests and pull the blessings down to earth for our kids. You can do the same!

Timing can be critical when it comes to standing in the gap for our kids. Dutch Sheets, author of *Intercessory Prayer*, has noted that the Bible uses two primary terms for *time*: *chronos*, meaning the actual time of day, and *kairos*, meaning "the right time," "the opportune time," or "the appointed time." Standing in the gap requires us to be on watch for our kids, sensitive to the timing of the Holy Spirit. Sometimes He will move us to pray for our kids during an *appointed time*, when they're facing a specific danger or temptation. He calls us to intercede (the Greek word *paga*) in order to set boundaries of spiritual and physical protection around our children. (*Paga* means "to meet, encounter, or reach.")

Sheets gives the following illustration of a Prayer Warrior Mom who powerfully stood in the gap for her son during a *kairos* ("appointed" or "opportune") time:

> I had a friend in Dallas several years ago who experienced an interesting answer to prayer in a *kairos* situation. She had gone early one morning to visit her son and daughter-in-law. The son worked an all-night shift so, awaiting his return from work, his wife and mother visited for a while.
>
> As time wore on and the son didn't arrive, Mom began to feel uneasy. Something didn't seem right. Thinking that perhaps he was still at work, they called his place of employment.
>
> "No," they were told, "he has already left."
>
> Becoming more alarmed, the mother said, "I'm concerned. Let's drive toward his place of work." She had assumed her son had left work at his normal time and should have been home by then when, in fact, he had left

just moments before their call. But the Lord was directing even in that because, though he was not in any danger yet, the Holy Spirit knew a *kairos* moment was coming for this young man, and He wanted this praying mother there when it happened.

As Mom and daughter-in-law drove toward his workplace on a busy Dallas parkway, they saw him coming from the other direction on his motorcycle, traveling around 40 to 50 miles per hour.

As they watched, he fell asleep and veered off the road, hit the curb, and flew 40 or 50 feet through the air. He was not even wearing a helmet. As the boy was moving through the air, Mom was praying, "Jesus, protect my son!"

She continued to pray as they turned around and drove back to him. A crowd had already gathered around him, and they ran to the scene wondering what they would find. They found a miracle! No injuries—no bones broken, no lacerations, no internal injuries. Just a dazed young man wondering what had happened. *Paga* happened . . . *Kairos paga* happened! Boundaries happened. A mother picked up on the warning from the Holy Spirit and was therefore in the right place at the right time.

Does this mean that if you weren't there praying when someone you loved had an accident, you're to blame for their injury or death? Of course not. If we all played that guessing game, it would drive us insane. It simply means we must be alert, and when warnings do come from the Holy Spirit, we must respond by praying—building some boundaries.[2]

Prayer walking is another excellent method that will help you enjoy some exercise while you intercede and stand in the gap for your children. I find that walking or exercising stimulates my mind as I pray, and I've also discovered that praying aloud while I walk keeps my prayers more focused. Prayer walking with your husband, your kids, another family member, or a friend provides a fun way to stay in shape and spend time together while interceding for your children.

In his book *The Circle Maker*, Mark Batterson illustrates the spiritual significance of setting goals and then making prayer circles around those goals, similar to the way the Israelite people walked thirteen times around the walls of Jericho before taking the city. He wrote:

> Jesus is on His way out of Jericho when two blind men hail Him like a taxi: "Lord, son of David, have mercy on us!" . . . Jesus stops and responds with a pointed question: *What do you want me to do for you?*
>
> Jesus forced them to define exactly what they wanted from Him—to verbalize their desire. He made them spell it out, but it wasn't because Jesus didn't know what they wanted; he wanted to make sure *they* knew what *they* wanted.
>
> Most of us have no idea what we want God to do for us. And that's why our prayers aren't just boring to us; they are uninspiring to God. Well-developed faith results in well-defined prayers, and well-defined prayers result in a well-lived life.
>
> Don't just read the Bible. Start circling the promises.

Don't just make a wish. Write down a list of God-glorifying life goals.

Don't just pray. Keep a prayer journal.

Define your dream.

Claim your promise.

Spell your miracle.

Jericho is spelled many different ways. If you have cancer, it's spelled *healing*. If your child is far from God, it's spelled *salvation*. If your marriage is falling apart, it's spelled *reconciliation*. If you have a vision beyond your resources, it's spelled *provision*.[3]

As I read the biblical account of the battle of Jericho, God illuminated two powerful truths within my spirit. First, He reminded me that the Israelites didn't even have to fight the so-called "battle" of Jericho. *God had already given them the victory*; they simply had to follow His instructions and take the city. Each day for six days they circled the city once. On the seventh day they circled the city seven times. Then they lifted up a mighty shout, and the walls of the city fell flat.

Second, the Lord brought to light a surprising aspect of the story. After the Israelites had taken the city, Joshua warned the people, "Cursed be the man before the Lord who rises up and builds this city Jericho; he shall lay its foundation with his firstborn, and with his youngest he shall set up its gates" (Josh. 6:26).

Sacrificing the firstborn—for me, that would be my son, Evan.

Sacrificing the youngest child—for me, that would be my daughter, Eden.

That's some serious stuff. When God tears down the walls

for us and our children, when He destroys the city built by our enemy, we must choose to live in a new place of victory. If we choose to live in the past and try to "rebuild the walls" of Jericho, we literally sacrifice the lives of our children.

Don't pick up bricks of fear and use them to rebuild the walls. Don't try to remake the past; you can't. Through the power of God, your Jericho is gone!

Years ago, I read the story of Carol Kent, an inspiring Prayer Warrior Mom. Her only child, Jason, was one of those seemingly "perfect" children: a straight-A student, well-mannered, a graduate of the U.S. Naval Academy in Annapolis who went on to become a Navy lieutenant. Jason married a sweet girl named April, who had two daughters, Chelsea and Hannah, from her first marriage. He loved those two girls as if they were his own.

However, over time, Jason grew concerned and agitated about his daughters spending time with their biological father, Douglas. Douglas had been abusive to April, and Jason suspected that he may have also sexually abused the girls. Douglas had begun seeking unsupervised visits with his daughters through the court system, and Jason grew worried about trying to protect the two girls.

One night, Jason drove to Orlando, Florida, where Douglas lived. He went out looking for Douglas and shot him dead in a parking lot. No one had suspected that this "model young man" could even be capable of such a shocking act.

Stunned, Carol and her husband, Gene, fought hard to stand in the gap for Jason. Carol recorded her family's journey through this ordeal in her book *When I Lay My Isaac Down*. In it she described the type of "Jericho prayer walks" that she felt led to take while her son awaited his trial:

We had made plans with April [my daughter-in-law] to do a Jericho-style prayer walk around the justice complex in Orlando before jury selection began. We did it twice in two-and-a-half years. The circular trip around that gigantic building took a long time, and we prayed fervently for the judge, the prosecutor, and J. P.'s attorneys. We asked God to protect Jason and to give him strength and wisdom; we prayed for his demeanor in the courtroom and for insight should there be a plea bargain offer even at this late date.

Carol and her family members fully believed the judge and jury would understand Jason's anguish over the abuse he felt that his daughters had experienced. They trusted and prayed that the jury would take into consideration Jason's military service, his character, and his spotless record of good conduct up to that point.

However, the courts sentenced Jason to life in prison. And in Florida, that sentence carries no possibility of parole.

Carol says, "Jason's sentence was an almost fatal blow to my faith. I couldn't understand why God would let this happen . . . *My* God was a rescuing God, a very present help in time of trouble, a God of miracles and second chances, a God who heard and answered prayer, a God of mercy and grace. I thought I had mountain-moving faith."[4]

No parent would ever choose to experience what Carol and her family did, but her story has empowered millions of hurting parents worldwide, encouraging them to fight the good fight even when they have to "lay their Isaacs down."

You see, Carol discovered that even in the worst

imaginable circumstances, God was still there. He still loved her. He still blessed and protected Jason, even in a prison cell. Carol, Gene, and Jason began a prison ministry called Speak Up for Hope that has enabled them to provide practical assistance and share the gospel with thousands of prison inmates and their families. God showed Carol that He had a purpose for Jason, even though He called this faithful mom to sacrifice on the altar the "perfect life plan" she had envisioned for her son.

For me, Carol's story became a watershed regarding how I perceive God and how I approach Him in prayer. You see, God's name is I AM; it's not I DO.

We sometimes approach prayer as though it's all about what God can do for us. But it's really about praising God for who He is. We must be willing to accept I AM even when He doesn't do what we think He should. We must be willing to accept the answer, "My grace is sufficient for you" (2 Cor. 12:9).

Carol's story also reminds me to be grateful for the blessing of every moment I spend with my son and daughter, to thank God for every day that I can talk to them and laugh with them, snuggle with them, read them stories, and run my fingers through their hair. Every day, I remind them that they are my "priceless treasure," and they are!

Take a Jericho Prayer Walk

Recently, I felt the Lord leading me to take a "Jericho prayer walk" to address some heart attitudes and emotions that seemed to be oppressing my spirit.

As I walked around my house seven times, I prayed, "Lord, I claim Your victory over these attitudes in the name of Jesus Christ. You have not given me a spirit of hopelessness, but You have taken my cloak of despair and draped me in a royal robe of praise. In the name of Jesus Christ, I bind Satan and will no longer allow him to influence my thoughts in these areas. Tear down the walls of these attitudes and never allow them to be rebuilt."

During my Jericho walk, I prayed for God to replace:

- my feelings of hopelessness with a spirit of "all joy and peace in believing" and give me a "garment of praise" in place of my "spirit of heaviness" (Rom. 15:13; Isa. 61:3).
- my fear and anger with a spirit of "power and of love and of a sound mind" (2 Tim. 1:7).
- my despair and depression with a spirit of hope and praise for God's help (Ps. 42:5).
- my feelings of victimization with a spirit of victory through Jesus Christ (1 Cor. 15:57).
- my chaos and disorder with "the wisdom from above," which is "pure, . . . peaceable, gentle, reasonable, full of mercy and good fruits, unwavering, [and] without hypocrisy" (James 3:17 NASB).
- my unforgiveness with a spirit of forgiveness based on my own forgiveness and redemption through the blood of Jesus, according to the riches of His grace (Eph. 1:7).
- my feelings of bitterness with a spirit of love and agreement by "letting all bitterness, wrath, anger, clamor, and evil speaking be put away" from me

and by being "kind to [others], tenderhearted, forgiving [them], even as God in Christ forgave [me]" (Eph. 4:31–32).

As I circled my house seven times, I prayed for God to lift my depression and to be fully present in my home and family. I prayed, "Lord, keep me and my children free, now and forever, from all these emotions and attitudes of defeat." As I cast these burdens on the Lord, I physically felt Him lift the spiritual weight of depression from me and strip the scales of pain from my eyes.

Suddenly I noticed little things that I hadn't seen before: small signs of hope, like a bird singing on a shrub in front of our house, and a neighbor's lavender lilacs exploding from her flower beds. When I walked around the garage to the left side of my house, I rejoiced to see the chartreuse shoots of several tulips springing up out of a pretty green flowerpot that I had thought was empty. And the Lord planted this passage from Isaiah in my mind:

> "Fear not, for I have redeemed you;
> I have called you by your name;
> You are Mine . . .
> I will bring your descendants from the east,
> And gather you from the west;
> I will say to the north, 'Give them up!'
> And to the south, 'Do not keep them back!'
> Bring My sons from afar,
> And My daughters from the ends of the earth . . .
> Do not remember the former things,

Nor consider the things of old.
Behold, I will do a new thing,
Now it shall spring forth;
Shall you not know it?
I will even make a road in the wilderness
And rivers in the desert." (Isa. 43:1, 5–6, 18–19)

Why not take a Jericho prayer walk today? Claim victory for your children by praying for God to tear down the walls built by the enemy. Ask the Lord to help you cultivate positive attributes, attitudes, and behaviors in their lives. Reflect on the "God-glorifying life goals"[5] that you want for yourself and your kids. Here are some excellent lists of principles to pray over during your Jericho prayer walk:

- Pray for your children to display the ninefold fruit of the spirit (love, joy, peace, patience, kindness, goodness, faithfulness, gentleness, and self-control).
- Pray for your children to develop a saving relationship with Christ as you pray over the seven "I AM" statements made by Jesus (I am the bread of life; I am the light of the world; I am the door; I am the good shepherd; I am the resurrection and the life; I am the way, the truth, and the life; I am the true vine[*]).
- Pray for your children to live godly, self-controlled lives and not to practice any of the following "deeds of the flesh": immorality, impurity,

---

[*] John 6:35; 8:12; 10:7, 9, 11; 11:25; 14:6; 15:1.

sensuality, idolatry, sorcery, enmities, strife,
jealousy, outbursts of anger, disputes, dissensions,
factions, envying, drunkenness, and carousing
(Gal. 5:19–21 NASB).

- Pray for your children to meditate and dwell
  on: "whatever is true, whatever is honorable,
  whatever is right, whatever is pure, whatever
  is lovely, whatever is of good repute, . . . [and]
  anything worthy of praise" (Phil. 4:8 NASB).
- Pray for your children to follow the Ten
  Commandments (Ex. 20).
- Pray for your children to display the godly
  attitudes in the Beatitudes (Matt. 5:3–12).

Will you do me a favor? Please let me know about the
details of your prayer walk and how you have seen God transform your life and the lives of your children. You can post to
my Prayer Warrior Mom website at www.PrayerWarriorMom
.com. I can't wait to hear about how the Lord uses prayer to
create "rivers in your desert" and replace your cloak of despair
with a beautiful garment of praise (Isa. 43:19; 61:3).

Today's Prayer

Dear Lord, teach me to storm Your throne with confident faith. Teach me to stand in the gap for my children, just as Jesus stood in the gap for me when my sin separated me from You, Father. I am visualizing the treasure chest of blessings that You've prepared for each one of my children [list their names here]. God, I pray that You will pour out Your spirit of blessing and provision on them. Meet all their needs according to Your holy will. Lead them in the paths of Your righteousness, and never allow them to stumble.

Lord, give me wisdom as I begin to take prayer walks with You. Rip down the walls of my city of Jericho, and never let them be rebuilt. Give me the faith to take the city, knowing You have already won the battle. Lord, today I claim Your victory over my Jericho [a major problem you are facing, or a positive goal for your life]. I thank You in advance for tearing down the walls that impede this goal. Destroy the barriers, and help me stake a claim in my children's godly future.

I ask You today to pour out blessings on my children [list any areas where they are facing challenges and obstacles]. I bind the power of Satan in their lives. Lord, bless them with Your mercy and grace. Make me an example of godly living. Make me an encourager, Lord. Help me to pray daily for Your Word, Your attributes, and godly attitudes to be implanted, developed, and matured in my children. In Jesus' holy name, amen.

The Sword of the Spirit

Put on the whole armor of God, that you may be able to stand against the wiles of the devil. (Eph. 6:11)

There is one God and one Mediator between God and men, the Man Christ Jesus, who gave Himself a ransom for all. (2 Tim. 2:5–6)

My little children, these things I write to you, so that you may not sin. And if anyone sins, we have an Advocate with the Father, Jesus Christ the righteous. (1 John 2:1)

Therefore we do not lose heart. Even though our outward man is perishing, yet the inward man is being renewed day by day. For our light affliction, which is but for a moment, is working for us a far more exceeding and eternal weight of glory, while we do not look at the things which are seen, but at the things which are not seen. For the things which are seen are temporary, but the things which are not seen are eternal. (2 Cor. 4:16–18)

Small Group Discussion Questions

1. In which areas do you feel the Lord leading you to stand in the gap for your children? Why do you feel your kids are particularly vulnerable in these areas? To you, what does it mean to stand in the gap for them?

2. What harmful attitudes and actions might God be leading you to sacrifice on the altar today? How do you think your life will change when you begin to walk in victory in these areas?

3. What are your greatest goals and dreams for your children? Lift them up to the Lord now.

4. How do you think Carol Kent's attitude about her son changed when she had to release her dreams for his future to the Lord?

5. Make a plan to embark on a prayer walk within the next week. During your personal prayer time over the next few days, journal about how your Jericho prayer walk might take shape. When and where will you walk? With a friend, or alone? Write down any attitudes, prayer needs, dreams, hopes, plans, issues, or anything else you want to address with God during that time. When you return from your walk, record how God spoke to you and ministered to your heart while you walked. Continue to take prayer walks as often as possible. Share the results with your husband and children.

4

Satisfy the Conditions
for Answered Prayer

Prayer is weakness leaning on omnipotence.

—W. S. BOWD[1]

GOD *ALWAYS ANSWERS PRAYER.* ALWAYS.

He either says, "Yes," "No," or "Wait."

Now, let me be clear here: He may not always answer our prayers the way we think He should. And He may not always give us what we ask for.

Aren't you glad?

Many times, I've asked for something from God and then later breathed a sigh of relief when He said no. But then, I've experienced other times when I desperately sought a "Yes" from Him, but my prayers seemed to fall on deaf ears. And I had to do a heart check to see if I was asking from a pure heart, with the right motives, according to His will.

Interestingly, several principles in the Bible indicate that our heavenly Father is more likely to honor certain prayers (both the requests and the individuals making them) with a "Yes" than others. Because we want to be Prayer Warrior Moms who live in constant communion with our Lord, let's do a heart check together and ask ourselves if we satisfy these conditions.

As you read through the list, ask the Holy Spirit to convict you of any conditions that may be causing a breach in your prayer life. At the end of the chapter, I'll lead you through a prayer that will help you confess and release any harmful attitudes or impure motives so you can clearly see, hear, and discern His will for you and your kids.

Most important, please keep in mind that God is a God of grace. He doesn't expect us to be perfect or to "get our act together" before He will answer our prayers. In His mercy, He honors the prayers of repentant sinners; otherwise, none of us would be able to have a relationship with Him.

These principles simply offer you food for thought and conviction, if the Holy Spirit leads. I hope they will inspire you to eliminate anything from your life that could hinder your intimate prayer dialogue with the Father.

My hope is that as you have begun to implement the prayers and principles in this book, you've already seen amazing progress and experienced remarkable breakthroughs in your prayer life. I hope you've reaped bountiful blessings as a result of covering each of your children with prayer. I've been *astonished* to see the spiritual, physical, emotional, and intellectual progress that God has effected in the lives of my children as I have prayed for them using the principles, scriptures, and prayers in this book. My daughter has blossomed into a beautiful young lady, and my son has developed such a sweet, caring spirit.

Do any of you have a testimony like that? If so, I rejoice with you. Please share your story with me and other readers on my website!

Now, I want to empower you to tear down any remaining barriers that may be keeping you and your children from experiencing God's absolute best for you every day. Let's align our lives with the conditions for answered prayer that God lays out for us in Scripture. Here are the "top ten":

1. *Approach God with an attitude of humble submission.*

James 4:7 reminds us to "submit to God." That means in *everything.* James linked our humility before the Father with God's choice to perform mighty works and miracles in our lives through prayer (vv. 3, 6, 10). The Bible also says that Jesus "when He had offered up prayers and supplications . . . to Him who was able to save Him from death . . . was heard because of His godly fear" (Heb. 5:7).

God loves to answer the prayers of devoted mothers. I believe He has high regard for Prayer Warrior Moms who kneel before His throne and say "Your will be done" with an attitude of humility and submission. We're at our most powerful when we're on our knees. Prayer is where the real action is!

2. Come to God with pure motives.

James 4:2–3 says, "You lust and do not have; so you commit murder. You are envious and cannot obtain; so you fight and quarrel. You do not have because you do not ask. You ask and do not receive, because you ask with wrong motives, so that you may spend it on your pleasures" (NASB).

When you pray for your children today, ask God to reveal any impure motives that might be hindering your prayers. Also, consider the types of blessings you tend to pray for. Are they mainly material, or are they primarily spiritual? Think about the reasons you are praying for certain blessings. Is it because you truly feel they are God's will for your kids, or are you simply asking God to provide what *you* want for your children? Is your focus on material blessings, earthly status and achievement, and things that indicate worldly success? Or is your concern for your children to pursue the heart of God and the values of His kingdom?

3. Don't ask for anything that contradicts God's Word.

When you pray for yourself and your children, guard against asking for anything that directly opposes or conflicts with God's principles as taught in Scripture.

For example, if your unmarried son approaches you about moving in with his girlfriend before marriage, do you need to pray and ask God if that is His will? Of course not. Be careful not to blur the lines of what God calls "good and acceptable" (Rom. 12:2). You are your children's guardian; your prayers and wisdom help keep them from making decisions that are not God's best for them. In cases where the "right thing" is not black-and-white, spend time in prayer with your children before helping them make a godly choice. When the next step is unclear, pray and wait!

4. Have faith without doubting.

James 1:6 says that we "must ask in faith without any doubting, for the one who doubts is like the surf of the sea, driven and tossed by the wind" (NASB). Of course, the Lord understands that we are frail; sometimes our pain causes us to doubt His love or His desire to answer a certain prayer. In that case, pray for God to increase your faith and erase your doubt. Sometimes you may need to cry out, "Lord, I believe; please help my unbelief!" just like the man in Mark 9:24, who brought his suffering son to Jesus. Pouring out His extraordinary compassion, Jesus healed that man's son; He will do the same for you when you bring Him your doubts and fears. Tell Him all your hurts as well as your aspirations, hopes, and dreams for your children, and then leave *everything* at the altar. He will replace your doubt and your burdens with a spirit of unwavering faith.

Ever noticed the contrast between being a "worrier" and being a "warrior"? What a difference those two little letters make! I've heard that worry is like a rocking chair—it gives you something to do, but it doesn't get you anywhere. One author has noted that there is nothing we can do about 70 percent of our worries:

What We Worry About

40% are about things that never happen.

30% are about the past—which can't be changed.

12% are about criticism by others, mostly untrue.

10% are about health, which gets worse with stress.

8% are about real problems that can be solved.[2]

Let God shoulder your doubts. He will take you from "worrier" status to "warrior" status today!

5. Be single-minded.

Pray for God to make you a single-minded woman. The book of James says this about a person who doubts God: "Let not that man suppose that he will receive anything from the Lord; he is a double-minded man, unstable in all his ways" (1:7–8). Later, James wrote, "Purify your hearts, you double-minded" (4:8).

What does it mean to be single-minded? It requires us to know who God is, to know who we are, and to rest in His provision. It means that our minds are clear and we have our priorities in order: that we elevate God, our husbands, and our children before our home, work, church, ministry, and outside responsibilities. And it means that we cast all our cares on Him the instant we hear that little voice of doubt scurrying through our minds (see 1 Peter 5:7).

I love the story of a single-minded widow in Scripture. Jesus told the following parable:

> Now He was telling them a parable to show that at all times they ought to pray and not to lose heart, saying, "In a certain city there was a judge who did not fear God and did not respect man. There was a widow in that city, and she kept coming to him, saying, 'Give me legal protection from my opponent.' For a while he was unwilling; but afterward he said to himself, 'Even though I do not fear

God nor respect man, yet because this widow bothers me,
I will give her legal protection, otherwise by continually
coming she will wear me out.'" (Luke 18:1–5)

This single-minded, persistent widow received her answer
from the judge, and that judge represents our heavenly Father.
Jesus indicated that because she prayed repeatedly and did not
lose heart, she was rewarded. That's the kind of woman I want
to be! How about you?

6. Pray for God's will to be done.

First John 5:14 says, "Now this is the confidence we have
in him, that if we ask anything according to His will, he hears
us." We can pray repeatedly for our children to receive a
certain blessing, but nothing will happen unless we pray for
God's will in that situation.

One author has written, "When we come to God, we have
to say, 'Your will be done.' And within those words resides
this meaning: 'If your will and my will are not in accord, then
I renounce my will in order that Your will may be done.'"[3]

I've often found myself humbled once I finally began to
pray, "God, please allow Your will to be done." At times, I've
been so sure about what I thought God was going to do that I
only prayed for that result. This happened once with my husband's job search. He had at least five interviews with a top
consulting firm, and we kept praying that he would get the job.
However, both of us were concerned about the detrimental
impact that the required travel might have on our family, especially our two small children.

Finally, one day, I heard the voice of the Holy Spirit

saying, "Pray for *My will* to be done." Whoops! I'd only been praying for my own will to be done. So I gave it all to God and finally prayed, "Lord, if it is Your will, please open the door for David to get this job. If not, please close the door so we can have peace about the decision."

The next day, he received a phone call from the VP of that company saying that he did not get the job. And the Lord revealed a better plan for us and our children. We could have saved a lot of heartache by praying for God's will from day one.

7. *Come boldly to His throne with confidence.*

Hebrews 4:16 says, "Let us therefore come boldly to the throne of grace, that we may obtain mercy and find grace to help in time of need." And John wrote, "Beloved, if our heart does not condemn us, we have confidence toward God" (1 John 3:21).

Sin, anger, and a root of bitterness can keep us from approaching God's throne with full confidence. If you have a feeling of heaviness, oppression, or alienation in your spirit, you cannot "come boldly" to the throne of grace. In that case, your sin and emotional pain have erected a wall between you and God. As you use prayer, fasting, and Scripture to remove the bricks from that wall of negative emotions, you will gain a sense of greater peace and connectedness with the Lord.

8. *Always pray to the Father, in the name of Jesus Christ, through the power of the Holy Spirit.*

The name of Jesus is the most powerful word we could ever speak. God has divinely given it to us for the destruction of fortresses (2 Cor. 10:4). The name "Jesus" literally means

"Yahweh saves." It's directly tied to our salvation: it reflects the blood that Jesus shed on the cross to save us from our sins and the resurrection, which gives us hope and eternal life.

The resurrection of Jesus Christ sets Him apart from every other spiritual leader in history. Because Jesus is crowned, victorious, and seated at the right hand of God in the heavenly realms, His name has both the ultimate power and the final authority in heaven and on earth. He is our Advocate before the Father, and His blood literally "speaks" in the heavenly realms (Heb. 12:24). Always pray in Jesus' name.

9. Confess and repent of your sin.

Have you ever felt as though your prayers were stopping at the ceiling? I have. At the time, I knew it was because my unconfessed sin and improper attitudes were robbing me of proper communion with the Father.

According to 1 Peter 3:7, the prayers of husbands can be hindered if they do not treat their wives with consideration, respect, and tenderness. Is it possible, then, that our prayers as wives might also be hindered if we do not offer the proper love, respect, and submission to our husbands? The Bible says, "Nevertheless let each one of you in particular so love his own wife as himself, and *let the wife see that she respects her husband*" (Eph. 5:33; emphasis added).

Believe me: I know that respecting our husbands can be difficult, especially when we don't agree with what they are saying or doing. The greatest challenge is to try to love and respect a husband and children who do not make us feel loved and respected in return. But God calls us to make the first move. He reminds us to respect and honor our husbands and kids *no matter what, for better or for worse, in sickness and in health, till death do us part.* You may need to confess and repent if you have been harboring a bitter and unforgiving spirit toward any member of your family.

If possible, starting tonight, begin to establish a new habit of praying together with your husband and/or your children before you go to sleep. This time of connection will give you the opportunity to discuss any challenging issues that have arisen throughout the day. It will also keep you from letting "the sun go down on your anger" (Eph. 4:26 NASB).

10. *Forgive others.*

If we want God to hear our prayers and forgive our own sin, we must offer the gift of forgiveness to others. In fact, forgiveness is so critical to the effectiveness of our prayers that Jesus emphasized it in the Lord's Prayer. He told His disciples, "For if you forgive men their trespasses, your heavenly Father will also forgive you. But if you do not forgive men their trespasses, neither will your Father forgive your trespasses" (Matt. 6:12, 14–15).

If you struggle with unforgiveness, you're not alone. I find it challenging sometimes too. I'm a very sensitive person, and when someone has wronged me, I usually struggle to let that individual back into my circle of trust. When someone seems unsafe or capable of hurting me, I usually place that person outside of the realm of the people I trust. I have to remind myself that God wants me to forgive others as Jesus has forgiven me. No matter what I do or how many times I fail Him, He always welcomes me back into His circle of love and trust.

Forgiving doesn't mean forgetting. It doesn't mean keeping

a person from experiencing the consequences of his or her sinful words or actions. And it doesn't mean that our relationship with that person returns to the way it was before. But it does mean that we choose to move on and not remain in a self-built prison of bitterness.

As you look back through these ten conditions for answered prayer, the thread of "trusting God" winds through them all. Isaiah 26:3 says:

> You will keep him in perfect peace,
> Whose mind is stayed on You,
> Because he trusts in You.

Being a Prayer Warrior Mom means we release control to our sovereign Father and trust Him with every aspect of our children's lives and well-being. That means giving Him our children's future, even though our dreams for our kids may not come to fruition within our lifetime. If you're burdened with concern for your prodigal son or daughter, can you pray every day of your life with faith that your prodigal will turn to God, even if that does not happen during your days on this earth?

Max Lucado has noted that "Jesus never turned a parent away."[4] Whenever a panicked mother or father approached Jesus, begging Him to heal a son or daughter, how did Jesus always respond? With compassion and grace. With words of kindness and comfort. Sometimes even with tears. The heart of the Father is a wellspring of covenant love and tender mercy. God longs to honor your prayers for your kids, Prayer Warrior Mom!

If you struggle to keep the faith as your prodigal strays far from God, please be encouraged that your prayers will never die or return void. They will live on and continue to create results on earth even after you and I have gone to be with the Lord. I believe that God will save your son or daughter and that you will see it, even if you view that moment from your perfect vantage point in heaven. In the meantime, I pray that the Lord will bathe your soul with His perfect peace.

Today's Prayer

Dear Lord, thank You for always answering prayer. Give me the vision and wisdom to accept your answer, whether it is "Yes," "No," or "Wait." Help me to trust that You have my kids' best interests at heart, even when I can't see what the final result will be. When I can't see Your hand, help me to trust Your heart. Give me a spirit of humility and submission. Build confident faith within me, Lord. Teach me to come boldly before Your throne, without even a bit of doubt. Make me an example of the kind of faith that blossoms like a mustard seed. Help me instill that mountain-moving faith in my kids, too, Lord.

Please make me a single-minded woman who stays the course and keeps the faith. I pray for Your will always to be done in my life and the lives of my kids. I'm thankful that I can pray to You in the all-powerful and victorious name of Jesus Christ. I claim salvation for myself and my children in Jesus' name.

Give me a spirit of forgiveness and grace as I interact with others, Lord. Grant me patience with my children, the kind of patience that You shower onto me. Bind any spirit of anger, unforgiveness, and bitterness, and keep it from interfering with my relationship with my husband and children. Pour out Your perfect peace and blessing on me, my husband, my children, and our home. In Jesus' name, amen.

The Sword of the Spirit

You shall weep no more.
He will be very gracious to you at the sound of your cry;
When He hears it, He will answer you. (Isa. 30:19)

"And whatever you ask in My name, that I will do, that the Father may be glorified in the Son." (John 14:13)

And whatever we ask we receive from Him, because we keep His commandments and do those things that are pleasing in His sight. (1 John 3:22)

Small Group Discussion Questions

1. Do you believe God always answers prayer? Give examples of times when He has given you answers of "Yes," "No," and "Wait." What did you learn in each of those situations? When He said "No," did that turn out to be a blessing in disguise?

2. Are there certain situations that you have been praying about for weeks, months, or even years regarding your children? If so, what are they? Why do you think the Lord may be waiting to answer these prayers?

3. What lessons do we learn about God, ourselves, and our children when we have to wait for the Lord to answer our prayers? How do we change?

4. How might your situation change if you were to pray, "God, may Your will be done in this circumstance"?

5. Now that you have learned about the ten conditions for answered prayer, in which of the ten areas do you feel you may need to make some changes? Do you feel the Holy Spirit convicting you of any sinful heart attitudes? If so, confess them now, either in prayer to Him or to a friend in your Prayer Warrior Mom group.

5

Pray with Power and Authority

We and the world, my children, will always be at war.
Retreat is impossible.
Arm yourselves.

—LEIF ENGER[1]

ARCHIMEDES ONCE SAID, "GIVE ME A LEVER LONG enough and a fulcrum on which to place it, and I shall move the earth." Prayer is the "lever" we press on earth that unleashes God's power from heaven. It's the catalyst that moves God to enter into the earthly realm and act in tangible ways that we can measure in physical time and space. The results of our prayers may be miraculous and unexplainable by science or reason, but they are absolutely real.

God created the natural world to operate according to ordered, natural laws. In the same way, He created the spiritual world to operate according to His spiritual laws, set forth in His unfailing Word. Our seemingly simple prayers actually create a "heavenly reaction" that engages spiritual powers on a universal scale.

As Prayer Warrior Moms, we're called to teach our children to engage in spiritual warfare. The Bible says that our battle is not against flesh and blood, but against "principalities, against powers, against the rulers of the darkness of this age, against spiritual hosts of wickedness in the heavenly places" (Eph. 6:12). Therefore we must teach our kids to pray, and we must arm them to do battle against the forces of darkness.

The above passage highlights two critical truths: (1) we are in the fight of our lives; and (2) our battle is not against other people but against satanic forces. Yet sometimes we feel so hurt, disappointed, and blinded by sin and pain that we feel as if we are fighting *against* our husbands, our children, our family, and our friends. That is a ploy of Satan. He wants us to think that other people are our enemy, not him. Corrie ten Boom once said, "It's a poor soldier indeed who fails to recognize the enemy."[2]

Down here in Texas, I've met many precious Southern belles who never get a hair out of place. One of my friends says she doesn't sweat; she "glistens." But if we're going to get real with God, we have to *wrestle* with Him in prayer. We have to get our knees dirty if we're going to wage the kind of warfare that will rout Satan. God will bless us when we tear down the facade and wrestle, *really wrestle*, until we have put the powers of darkness into a choke hold.

One commentator has written, "We are not engaged in a human, physical warfare . . . It is a contest between two opponents that continues until one hurls the other one down and holds him down. The word *against* presents the idea of a personal foe, face-to-face and hand-to-hand conflict to the finish, a life and death struggle. Paul is not describing a Sunday School picnic."[3]

Most Christians are clueless about the deadly serious nature of spiritual warfare. For many years, I was too. When I enrolled in seminary and began training to enter the ministry, the intensity of my battle increased significantly. Now that I'm a full-time author and speaker with two children, the spiritual stakes have risen exponentially.

Every day, I'm just so blessed by people, and women in particular. My passion is to help every woman break through to blessing and experience the fullness of Christ's love, joy, freedom, and acceptance in her life. God has called me to help women stop striving so hard for perfection and instead, to learn to find peace and rest in the comfort of God's covenant love.

Aren't God's people amazing creations? In my travels and my speaking ministry, I enjoy meeting people from all walks of life, laughing and crying with them, and hearing their incredible stories. God has shown me a vital lesson: I have something fascinating to learn from everyone. My heart's desire is to be able to share biblical words of encouragement, blessing, and hope with every person that I meet. Sometimes my readers or audience members suffer from hurts that run so deep that theology doesn't salve the wound; then we just hug and cry together.

Sure, Satan tries to mislead me by reminding me of my faults and failures, but I refuse to allow him to win. I remind

Satan that Jesus wants every woman to live in victory. I tell him, "Back off. Jesus in me is the hope of glory!"

You will find that, as your spiritual influence and wisdom increase, so will Satan's attacks on you and your family. You and I have to stay on our knees in order to stay in the game! However, I want to assure you that you have nothing to fear. Remember that "God has not given us a spirit of fear" (2 Tim. 1:7). Some of us mistakenly believe that we're on the defensive, weakly trying to fight back against Satan's schemes. In fact, we are leading the charge. We're on the offensive. Get out of that foxhole, and get out there on the front lines, Prayer Warrior Mom! Suit up with the full armor of God, equipped to do battle.

To wage full-scale war against Satan, we must pray with both the *power* and the *authority* granted to us by God. Look again at Archimedes' statement; the lever is the power of God, and the fulcrum is our Savior, Jesus Christ, in whose holy name we have spiritual authority.

We often use the terms *power* and *authority* interchangeably, but they aren't exactly the same. Power is physical and relational; authority is legal and positional. One author wrote, "The Greek word translated as 'authority' is *exousia,* and its basic meaning is 'to have the right to rule or govern, as one whose will and commands ought to be submitted to and obeyed.' In contrast, the Greek word translated 'power' is *dunamis,* which means 'to have the inherent strength or actual ability to bring about a desired purpose.'"[4] Just because a person has the right to perform a certain act doesn't necessarily mean he or she has the power to carry it out.

I once worked with a lovely, petite young woman named Rachel, who was a Dallas police officer. She might not strike you as a "powerful" person at first glance, but when she walked up to you, sporting her police uniform, you definitely respected her authority. Her authority to uphold the law has been granted to her by an even higher authority—the Constitution of the United States of America.

Let's say that my friend Rachel is in uniform directing traffic at a busy intersection as a semi truck approaches. If she signals the truck driver to stop, will he stop? Probably. (I hope so, for his sake!) Physically, Rachel may not be more *powerful* than the truck or its driver, but she has *authority* over both truck and driver.

Jesus, on the other hand, has *both* the ultimate power and the ultimate authority over everything in heaven and earth. This enables Him to, among other things:

- forgive sins (Matt. 9:6)
- heal sickness, blindness, paralysis, and other physical ailments (Matt. 9:35)
- cast out demons (Matt. 8:28–34)
- sit at the right hand of God the Father (Matt. 26:64)
- raise the dead (John 11)
- walk on water and command the natural world (Matt. 14:25; Mark 4:39)
- destroy all schemes of the enemy (Luke 10:19)
- lay down His life and take it up again (John 10:18)
- do good and heal all who are oppressed by the devil (Acts 10:38)
- open people's eyes and turn them from the power of Satan to God (Acts 26:18)
- rise from the dead (Matt. 28:6)

- give us hope (2 Thess. 2:16)
- purchase our salvation (2 Tim. 2:10)

One author has written, "For effective prayer, there are two things we need: authority and power. To have authority we must have confidence that we have fulfilled all the legal requirements . . . Praying in the name of Jesus sets the seal of His authority on our prayers."[5]

Jesus said, "If you ask anything in My name, I will do it" (John 14:14). Always use the mighty name of Jesus to "set His seal" on your prayers for your kids. His holy name is just one of the seven powerful weapons of warfare that we have at our disposal. Here is our arsenal of spiritual weapons. I call it our "tower of power":

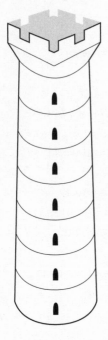

The name of Jesus Christ

The blood of Jesus Christ

Agreement with the Holy Spirit and other believers

Binding and loosing (forbidding the power of Satan and claiming victory through the Word of God)

Fasting

Praise and thanksgiving

The Word of God and the testimony of believers

These spiritual weapons work in contrast with the carnal weapons mentioned in Scripture, which are the mind (human reasoning), the soul (human desire), the will of man, manipulation, deception, and control.[6]

When you engage your "tower of power," you connect the power and authority of God with your children's needs on earth, swinging open the doors of blessing for you and your children. These weapons also break the curse of sin (both personal and generational) in your life and the lives of your kids.

Remember that no matter how fierce the battle gets, Satan is overpowered and outnumbered. When he fell, only a third of the angels fell with him (Rev. 12:4). That means you and I have God and two-thirds of the holy angels on our side! Remind your kids of that whenever they feel discouraged.

When you pray against the powers of darkness, be sure to pray in specifics. Author Mark Batterson has written, "The pastor of one of the largest churches, Seoul, Korea, wrote, 'God does not answer vague prayers.' When I read that statement, I was immediately convicted by how vague my prayers were. In fact, some of them were so vague that I had no way of knowing whether God had even answered them or not."[7]

Especially when we're fighting spiritual warfare, we must pray specifically, and we must pray Scripture for our kids. Here's an excellent sample prayer:

Lord, I claim victory for my children in the name of Jesus, at which every knee will bow. I claim salvation for them through the blood of Jesus Christ. By the authority of Jesus, I bind Satan and break any and all of his power over my children. I loose my children from Satan's hold. Keep them in godly territory. In agreement with Your Spirit, I destroy all strongholds of sin and all the works of the enemy in the lives of my children. I ask that You perform mighty works in their lives. Give them a glorious future and a powerful hope that will never be destroyed. In Jesus' name, amen.

Think about each of your kids and the struggles he or she faces today. What battle is each of them fighting? How are they growing? How do you think that Satan is trying to tempt, discourage, and mislead them? Write each child's name in your prayer journal, along with his or her primary struggle. Pray for your kids every day.

Recently, as I wrote the word *authority* in my journal, I noticed something I'd never observed before: it begins with the word *author*. Hebrews 12:1–2 says,

> Let us lay aside every weight, and the sin which so easily ensnares us, and let us run with endurance the race that is set before us, *looking unto Jesus, the author and finisher of our faith,* who for the joy that was set before Him endured the cross, despising the shame, and has sat down at the right hand of the throne of God. (emphasis added)

Running a good race requires us to lay aside the weight, the hurt, the depression, the anxiety, and the sin we may be carrying. Jesus has the power to speak calm into our chaos and create a godly design out of our disorder. He can help us pull our personal lives, our marriages, our homes, and our kids' lives into order.

Is your home a place of beauty, order, and delight? Is your relationship with your children characterized by love, joy, patience, peace, and creativity? Do you give your husband the best you have to offer, or does he receive the leftovers at the end of the day? Many of us are not living victoriously in these areas. We are letting Satan get a toehold in our lives. One of my good friends says, "Toehold, foothold, stronghold, stranglehold!"

When we live in the power and authority of Jesus, we avoid being lackadaisical wives and "wishbone parents." A "wishbone parent" is one who simply *wishes* her children would behave better. Maureen Healy wrote, "These parents have the best of intentions but don't do the things, like applying consistent discipline, that are necessary."[8]

I don't want to be a wishbone mom, whether that applies to parental discipline or my prayer life. Being an optimist and an idealist by nature, I've spent a lot of my life wishing for things that have never happened. Wishing doesn't get us very far, does it?

Let's pick up our power tools and move from the realm of wishful thinking to the realm of getting it done through the power of the Holy Spirit.

Today's Prayer

Dear Lord, today, I claim spiritual victory for my children. You already consider it done according to Your will. Thank You for giving me and my children power and authority through the name and the blood of Jesus Christ. Bless and protect my children in the areas of their health, their spirituality, their choice of friends, their studies, their career selection, their choice of a spouse, and all their pursuits. In the name of Jesus, I bind all evil spirits and command Satan to stay far away from my children.

Lord, help my children to always obey Your Word and Your commands. Protect them from physical, spiritual, and emotional harm. Keep them from developing a spirit of fear, bitterness, or insecurity. Teach them to discern and pursue Your will for them in everything. Give them a spirit of wholeness, confidence, triumph, and confidence in You. Help them to seek You, know You, and love You always. I pray that they will walk with You every day in victory. In Jesus' name, amen.

The Sword of the Spirit

God has not given us a spirit of fear, but of power and of love and of a sound mind. (2 Tim. 1:7)

The weapons of our warfare are not carnal but mighty in God for pulling down strongholds, casting down arguments and every high thing that exalts itself against the knowledge of God, bringing every thought into captivity to the obedience of Christ. (2 Cor. 10:4–5)

We do not wrestle against flesh and blood, but against principalities, against powers, against the rulers of the darkness of this age, against spiritual hosts of wickedness in the heavenly places. (Eph. 6:12)

But thanks be to God, who gives us the victory through our Lord Jesus Christ. (1 Cor. 15:57)

Small Group Discussion Questions

1. Satan's goal is to distract and mislead you and your children from attaining God's will for your lives. How does this truth affect your commitment to your prayer life? How does it change your prayers for your children?

2. Describe the difference between spiritual power and spiritual authority. How can you leverage both the power and the authority granted to you by Jesus Christ to achieve spiritual victory in your life?

3. Have you ever approached your husband, children, in-laws, boss, or others as though your battle were against them rather than against Satan, his demons, and the principalities of darkness? How does it help you to know that your battle is not against flesh and blood but against the spiritual forces of wickedness?

4. Take your prayer journal and define your personal life goals as well as your goals and dreams for each of your children for the coming calendar year. List the steps needed for each of you to reach those goals. How can you encourage your children to pursue their passions through the power and authority of Jesus Christ?

6

Get Help When You Need It

I don't need easy; I just need possible.

—BETHANY HAMILTON, AWARD-WINNING
SURF PHENOMENON AND INSPIRATION
FOR THE MOVIE *SOUL SURFER*

EVERY MOM NEEDS HELP.

All of us have weaknesses, sin patterns, bad habits, and tendencies that require us to lean on the Lord for strength each day. We also need to be able to lean on each other as sisters in the faith. Because of your great responsibilities, you need to be healthy and whole. Your kids need a Prayer Warrior Mom who can actively engage in battle for them.

Author Ann Voskamp, in an attempt to describe her struggle with depression, wrote:

> For years of mornings, I have woken wanting to die. Life twists itself into nightmare. For years, I have pulled the covers up over my head, dreading to begin another day I'd just wreck . . . I lie listening to the taunt of names ringing off my interior walls . . . *Loser. Mess. Failure.* They are signs nailed overhead, nailed through me, naming me. The stars are blinking out.
>
> . . . I wake to the discontent of life in my skin. I wake to self-hatred. To the wrestle to get it all done, the relentless anxiety that I am failing . . . I yell at children, fester with bitterness, forget doctor appointments, lose library books, live selfishly, skip prayer, complain, go to bed too late, neglect cleaning the toilets. I live tired. Afraid. Anxious. Weary . . . I feel it in the veins, the pulsing of ruptured hopes. Would I ever be enough, find enough, do enough?[1]

Ann is a loving wife, a devoted mother who homeschools her six children, a gifted author, and so much more. Yet Satan still tries to attack her and make her feel worthless and insignificant.

One of Ann's friends challenged her to keep a gratitude journal, in which she recorded one thousand things she was thankful for. As Ann began to view her life through the lens of thanksgiving, her black cloud of depression and discontentment began to lift. Her book *One Thousand Gifts* offers a poignant, uplifting account of how God changed her life and helped heal her emotional wounds through her expressions of gratitude.

Like Ann, you may be struggling with depression, illness, or another condition that keeps you from living victoriously. I believe God wants you to hear this message today from Isaiah 41:13:

> For I, the LORD your God, will hold your
> right hand,
> Saying to you, "Fear not, I will help you."

As soon as you are able, ask a family member, friend, or babysitter to watch your children so you can take a couple of hours to rest, pray, and recharge. Write in your prayer journal and your gratitude journal. Carve out some time for prayer and thanksgiving; create a respite amid the chaos. When you and I take time for ourselves, our children benefit. Our husbands benefit. And we benefit.

Maybe you're suffering from an abusive situation or an addiction today. Getting help may not be easy, but it's *possible*. Pray for God to grant you the hope and the strength to get help. Getting out of an abusive or addictive situation requires motivation. The healing process typically involves counseling and other forms of assistance, and getting better takes time too. Getting help requires you to be a visionary, to take that first step of faith, believing that your future *must* be better than your past.

Speaking of time, did you realize that *time alone does not heal anything*? Most of our wounds require much more than time to heal. You deserve to get well. You and your children deserve to live in peace and safety. You deserve to live the rest of your life in spiritual victory rather than despair.

Not only that, but you are *responsible* to get well. You love your family, and they need you. Clearly, Satan wants to keep you on the sidelines, but *God wants you on the front lines.* He wants you to become a more positive, joyful, and spiritually healthy Prayer Warrior Mom.

Following are several important (and free) resources for you.

- For women suffering from postpartum depression (PPD):
    - Contact the National Coalition of Mental Health at 1-866-8COALITION.
    - A helpful PPD website: Out of the Valley Ministries at postpartumprogress.com. The author of this blog lists postpartum health treatment centers in every state. Click on the tab "Get Help" on her homepage, and then select "PPD Treatment Programs."
    - Here are two helpful books for those suffering from postpartum depression: 1) *Living Beyond Postpartum Depression: Help & Hope for the Hurting Mom & Those Around Her* by Jerusha Clark. 2) *The Lifter of My Head: How God Sustained Me During Postpartum Depression* by Sue McRoberts.
- For free counseling from the Focus on the Family Help Center: call 1-855-771-4357.
- For abused women and children: call the National Domestic Violence Hotline at 1-800-799-7233.
- For abused women and children in the Dallas/ Fort Worth area: contact the Hope's Door domestic violence shelter at 1-972-422-7233.

- For women with suicidal thoughts: call the Suicide Hotline at 1-800-784-2433.
- For a teen counseling hotline: call 1-888-747-TEEN.
- For Teen Hope, offering biblical help for youth in crisis: call 1-800-HIT-HOME.
- For women dealing with self-injury and cutting: call the SAFE Hotline at 1-800-366-8288.
- For questions about spirituality and salvation: call Need Him at 1-800-NEED-HIM.

I pray that these resources will provide a first step for you in getting the help you need. I believe so strongly that today is your day to begin healing that I'm going to ask you to do something radical: *put this book down, get your phone out, and call for help.*

Congratulations! I'm proud of you for taking that crucial step.

During the writing of this book, I've been encouraged by the song "Overcome" by Christian recording artist Jeremy Camp, based on Revelation 12:10–11:

The accuser of our brethren has been thrown down, he who accuses them before our God day and night. And *they [believers] overcame him because of the blood of the Lamb and because of the word of their testimony.* (NASB, emphasis added)

Satan, your accuser, has been thrown down. You have overcome him with the blood of Jesus and your testimony of faith. Are you living like an overcomer, or are you "down for the count"?

If you've been down for the count, I empathize with you. I've been there. I understand the myriad challenges of trying to explain your depression or emotional pain to your husband, family, or friends. When I struggled with postpartum depression, I heard several of the following statements. You may have heard them too:

- "God doesn't want you to be depressed [or addicted, or sick]."
- "All new moms are sad and stressed-out; this is normal. You'll be fine."
- "If you just stop thinking negative and destructive thoughts, you'll feel better."
- "Snap out of it; your baby [and your husband, and your other children] needs you."
- "So many people have it worse off than you do. You should be thankful."
- "This should be the happiest time of your life."
- "Your baby is beautiful and healthy; you should be happy."
- "*You're* the one who wanted to have a baby. Why aren't you excited about it?"
- "If you had prayed hard enough [or had enough faith, or not committed such-and-such a sin], this wouldn't have happened to you."
- "If you were a stronger [or more resilient, or more spiritual] person, you would not be struggling with this issue."
- "You have a wonderful husband [and/or beautiful children, a lovely home, a good job,

and so forth]. What do you have to be depressed about?"

- "Maybe you were just not cut out to be a mother."
- "You must be going crazy. It's not normal for a mother to feel this way [or say these things, or act this way]."
- "Women have been having babies for thousands of years. What's the big deal? Why is it so difficult for you?"
- "Once you start getting more sleep [or exercising, losing weight, changing your diet, taking vitamins, going back to work, reading your Bible, praying more, etc.], you will feel better."
- "If you stopped [working outside the home, breastfeeding, etc.], you would be fine."
- "Maybe you should just put your kids into foster care."

I weep for you if your cries for help have fallen on deaf ears. I pray that, with the Lord's assistance, you will take the responsibility to pursue your own healing. I recognize that your pain is real. At their roots, depression and anxiety are not "spiritual" problems, though they can affect our spiritual lives. Depression and anxiety have well-documented mental, chemical, psychological, physical, and emotional causes.

Most important, if you are struggling with one or more of these conditions, please remember that *it is not your fault*. I believe that you will get well and that your healing, like mine, will be a win-win for everyone in your family and your circle of influence.

I realize now that I've suffered from cycles of depression since college, but I was stubborn, believing the lie that "spiritual people don't get depressed." I wanted to be the perfect wife and mom, the godly example, the spiritual woman who had it all together all the time. People looked to me as a model of Christianity, and I didn't want to let them down. In addition, my husband (the "realist") did not know how to help me, and he did not encourage me to seek treatment.

John Lennon once said, "When you're drowning, you don't say, 'I would be incredibly pleased if someone would have the foresight to notice me drowning and come and help me,' you just scream."[2]

But most of us don't even scream. I know I didn't. We just suffer silently.

Mary Beth Chapman, the wife of Christian recording artist Steven Curtis Chapman, wrote, "People who don't know much about depression often think of it as great sadness, and while it is that, it is so much more. I was sad, mad, frustrated, fearful, reclusive, critical, overwhelmed, and hopeless. No one wants all these adjectives . . . and certainly no one wants to live with a person who's experiencing them."

Finally, Mary Beth sought medical help. After testing her, Mary Beth's doctor said, "I don't know if you're familiar with the term 'clinical depression,' but I believe you've suffered from it for a long time."

Mary Beth continued:

It was a relief to know that what I suffered from had a name, [but] at the same time, I felt guilty and ashamed.

Like everything was my fault. I had no logical reason to be depressed. I had a wonderful, loving, faithful husband and healthy, great kids. We were financially blessed. I wasn't living in poverty, persecution or pain.

. . . What I found is that my depression actually became an opportunity to acknowledge to God that He was literally my only hope. In the darkest, loneliest times in the middle of the night, I realized that Christ is truly all I have. I realized that everything else—everything—is fleeting.[3]

Benjamin Franklin said, "The definition of insanity is doing the same thing over and over again and expecting different results." But isn't it easy for us to get into a rut and stay there, especially with all our responsibilities of caring for our husbands, children, and homes?

To get well, you must break the cycle. You must begin to live life differently.

Jesus illustrated this by often asking people this pointed question: *"Do you want to get well?"*

John 5 describes a man who spent every day lying beside the pool of Bethesda, waiting for someone to put him into the pool so he could get well. He had been ill for thirty-eight years.

When Jesus saw the man lying there, He had compassion on him. "Do you want to get well?" He asked the man.

The sick man answered, "Sir, I have no man to put me into the pool when the water is stirred up, but while I am coming, another steps down before me."

Jesus said to him, "Get up, pick up your pallet and walk." Immediately the man became well, and picked up his pallet and began to walk. That was the Sabbath, but Jesus didn't care. He granted the man a miracle—a new lease on life.

In her book *Come Closer*, Jane Rubietta has written:

Sometimes the honest answer to Jesus's question, "Do you wish to get well?" is, "Not really. Not so much; not too badly." As long as we aren't well, we have an excuse. We don't have to participate fully in the course presented to us or the options available; we make allowances, not expecting as much of ourselves but expecting more of others. Not being well provides us with unhealthy opportunities for self-indulgence, mollycoddling, and grasping for attention. Maybe the unwellness is anger, bitterness, unforgiveness, anxiety over relationships, or some other means of keeping people at arm's length.

Sin makes us unwilling to come to the Author of life. When I relish the brick and mortar I stack between myself and another, hoping my distance and isolation strategy will garner attention and sorrow on another's part, I sin. And part of me dies. Because any time I move away from relationships, I move toward death. And away from Jesus.[4]

In Luke 19:9, Jesus said, "Today salvation has come to this house." Today is the day for you to snap those heavy shackles and dance with joy before the Lord. Today is your day to unlock the cage of anger, addiction, and despair so you can soar free on wings like an eagle.

Help is always available, but *you need to ask for it*. Satan will make you think that no one cares, or that no one wants to help you; that is a lie from the pit of hell. Many people on this earth love you, and your life is of infinite value to God.

You may have tried to relate your needs to your husband, mother, father, a friend, a colleague, or someone at your church, and maybe that didn't work. Perhaps you are a single mom, or you live in an isolated area. Maybe you don't have any family nearby, and you have no one to watch your children so you can attend counseling.

No matter how dark your situation, you can at least tell someone (a pastor, friend, doctor, one of your parents, your husband, or even a distant family member) that you need help. If you don't have the energy to seek help for yourself, please ask someone to get help *for* you.

I will be happy to connect you with Christian professionals who can encourage you, pray with you, and guide you on the path toward healing. On my website, www .PrayerWarriorMom.com, I offer a wide network of free and confidential Christian counseling services (some by phone) that can assist you in getting the help you need right away.

I understand how it feels to be under spiritual attack. As I type right now, I have scratches, bruising, and a large, greenish lesion under the skin of my left hand. Yesterday, I was playing outside in our backyard with my two children when I noticed that a thistle had sprung up. I reached down and pulled it up. No big deal, right? A few minutes later, I took the children inside, and I washed my hands in the bathroom sink.

My face began to flush as though I had eaten a bowlful of habañero peppers. Then my heart began beating strangely fast and erratically. I grabbed my phone, sat down on the couch, and called my husband. "I think I'm having an allergic reaction," I told him.

"Call 9-1-1," he said.

By the time I dialed 9-1-1, I could hardly speak. My brain and mouth felt completely disconnected. The dispatcher asked me my name and address. (Of course, both are very long!) She asked me to spell them, which I did laboriously. Then she asked, "Can you get up and go unlock the front door?" I looked at the door; when had it moved? Suddenly it was a mile away!

I struggled to stand up, and I went and unlocked it. I staggered back to the edge of the carpet, sank down, and passed out. I assume the 9-1-1 dispatcher was still on the line. I have no idea how long I was out.

Wake up.

Wake up, whispered a still, small voice through my disoriented mind.

The Holy Spirit must have spoken these words to me, because suddenly I woke up. I had no idea who I was, where I was, or what had happened. I was lying on my left side, with a strange, sideways view of my hallway, as if I had stumbled into a carnival fun house. (I discovered later that mental confusion is one of the symptoms of this type of allergic reaction.)

I could feel something in my left hand; I looked over and saw my phone. Despite the haze clouding my mind, I remembered that I had been on the phone with 9-1-1.

Just then, the front door flew open and the paramedics rushed in. They gave me an epinephrine shot in my left arm and rushed me to the hospital. I had gone into anaphylactic shock from my exposure to the allergens in the thistle and the fire ant bites.

Now, is that bizarre or what? Please keep in mind that I have no allergies of any kind—not one. I have had multiple bee stings and bug bites and have never had any type of allergic reaction to any of them.

After my near-death scare, Satan didn't even wait a day to launch a secondary attack on me. The day after my hospital stay, as my husband was helping me transfer and back up some of my files containing the chapters of this book, the folder containing the *entire first half of the book* disappeared. Eight chapters.

At first, I was in shock. *This can't be happening*, I thought. We tried again and again to open the file. Nothing.

I slumped my head on my desk and sobbed. That was one of the worst moments of my entire life. I had poured my heart and soul into those chapters. I felt that there was no way I could re-create them exactly the way they had been before. I also felt scared that I would not be able to finish the book in time after losing that much material. And I still felt exhausted and out of sorts from the effects of the allergic reaction.

A spirit of depression and despair settled on me for the next few days. I couldn't bear the thought of having to sit down and rewrite hundreds of pages of material. During that time, I continually prayed to the Lord, asking for renewed strength and inspiration. I asked Him for the grace to "write off" those eight chapters of the book and release them to Him. I begged for the physical and emotional energy to begin again and to write truer, more passionately, and with more power the words that He wanted me to say.

To be honest, I had a large-scale pity party. My focus was still on myself and the pain of my loss. I prayed, "God, please help me. Help me be able to remember and retype what I lost. Help me minister to my readers. If there are new insights You want me to include, please give them to me. Make the new version better than before."

Later that day I was in the kitchen, when the voice of the Holy Spirit sent this Scripture verse (which is also a lyric from a song sung by Steve Green) straight and true like an arrow through my mind: *"He who began a good work in you will be faithful to complete it"* (Phil 1:6, paraphrased; emphasis added).

Hmmm.

I pondered that for a moment.

"He who began a good work in you will be faithful to complete it."

Emphasis on the "He."

Oh . . . Okay, Lord. Now it's clear.

In other words, *"Marla, you cannot complete it. But I can complete it. Give it all to Me. Let Me write the book through you."*

Now, as I type, my heart is in a completely different place after dealing with those two gut-wrenching trials. More than ever, I know God is faithful. He is in control. His Holy Spirit is *within* me, and He is *with* me. On God's timeline, the book is already finished and creating miraculous results in heaven and on earth.

In fact, in a strange way, I felt encouraged by the fact that Satan was trying so hard to keep this book from being written. That confirmed to me that God is going to use *Prayer Warrior Mom* to empower many moms to pray with courage and faith for their kids. It renewed my confidence that He will use the prayers and principles in this book to help you break through to blessing and see God perform miracles in your children's lives.

Satan will fight hard, but God has already won, my friends. I can't promise you a life free of pain and hardship. But I can promise you a life of hope through Jesus Christ—hope like a megawatt lighthouse beacon that cuts through even the darkest night and the thickest fog. He is healing me, and I know He will heal you too.

Shauna Niequist wrote:

There are things that happen to us, and when they happen, they give us two options. Either way, we will never be the same, and we shouldn't. These things can either strip us down to the bone and allow us to become strong and honest, or they can be the reasons we use to behave poorly indefinitely, the justification for all manner of broken relationships and broken ideals. It could be the thing that allows everything else to turn, that allows the lock of our lives to finally spring open and our pent-up selves to blossom like preening flowers. Or it can be the reason we use to justify our anger and the sharp tones in our voices for the rest of our lives.

Celebration when you think you're calling the shots? Easy. Celebration when your plan is working? Anyone can do that. But when you realize that the story of your life could be told a thousand different ways, that you could tell it over and over as a tragedy, but you choose to call it an epic, that's when you start to learn what celebration is. When what you see in front of you is so far outside of what you dreamed, but you have the belief, the boldness, the courage to call it beautiful instead of calling it wrong, that's celebration.[5]

I pray that you will begin to celebrate your life as an epic today. I hope you'll arm yourself well for battle and surround yourself *now* with other praying women who love you and will support you. Start a Prayer Warrior Mom group at your church, and pray faithfully with those women. I structured this book with fifteen chapters so it can be used for a semester-long or summer Bible study. Please let me know personally how God is working in your life and the lives of your children. I can't wait to hear from you!

God sees you as worthy to fight on the front lines, and He has equipped you with every weapon you need to win. Your prayers for your children are already channeling a mind-boggling amount of power from heaven down to earth. You are the superconductor, bringing God's will down from heaven and plugging it into the circle of your family on earth. Your heavenly Father says:

"Surely, as I have thought, so it shall come to pass,
And as I have purposed, so it shall stand."
    (Isa. 14:24)

Today's Prayer

Dear Lord, I need Your help. I've been carrying a burden of [sadness, depression, stress, pain, addiction, or (fill in the blank)] for a long time now. I am ready to get help. I don't want to live like this anymore. I want to live in victory. I claim Your healing today. I claim today, _____ , as the beginning of my journey toward wellness. I believe that You have a plan to prosper my future and bless my children far beyond what I can even ask or imagine.

Lord, I believe You can do this; please help my unbelief. Increase my faith when it is weak. Give me the motivation to seek help. I desperately need a fresh infusion of Your grace. I long for the safety and security that only You can provide. I crave a home where peace, patience, and love abound. Make me an instrument of Your peace in my family. Teach me to model patience and triumphant faith. Give me a name, a place where I can find help. Open a door for me. Please bring someone into my life who can help me. Give me a "divine appointment."

Grant me the motivation and energy to obtain help and healing for myself and my children. I thank You in advance for Your healing. I believe You have already seen my healing come to pass through the power of Your Spirit. I believe You also have granted my children wholeness, healing, peace, and security. In Jesus' name, I bind Satan and I cast off his evil plans for me and my children. He will never win over me. I cast off the spirit of fear. Give me a sound mind and a victorious faith today. In Jesus' name, amen.

The Sword of the Spirit

Your light shall break forth like the morning,
Your healing shall spring forth speedily,
And your righteousness shall go before you;
The glory of the LORD shall be your rear guard. (Isa. 58:8)

I would have despaired unless I had believed that I would
see the goodness of the LORD in the land of the living.
(Ps. 27:13)

"But for you who fear My name, the sun of righteousness
will rise with healing in its wings; and you will go forth
and skip about like calves from the stall." (Mal. 4:2 NASB)

>Create in me a clean heart, O God,
>And renew a steadfast spirit within me. (Ps. 51:10)

"Until now you have asked nothing in My name. Ask, and
you will receive, that your joy may be full." (John 16:24)

>Arise, cry aloud in the night
>At the beginning of the night watches;
>Pour out your heart like water
>Before the presence of the Lord;
>Lift up your hands to Him
>For the life of your little ones. (Lam. 2:19 NASB)

>But You, O LORD, are a shield for me,
>My glory and the One who lifts up my head. (Ps. 3:3)

Small Group Discussion Questions

1. In what areas of your life do you need the most help today? List the top three.

2. What lies, discouraging words, and hurtful comments have you heard regarding these issues? Discuss them in your group if you feel comfortable and write them down. It's important for you to reflect on these so you can see the negative and self-destructive messages that Satan has been trying to send you. What false messages (or messages of guilt, blame, and shame) has Satan been sending you about these problems?

3. Now, think about the scriptures you have learned throughout this book and the spiritual truths you have discovered. Write out a positive, biblical answer to refute each of the negative messages.

4. Picture Jesus standing in front of you, asking, "Do you want to get well?" What would your answer be? What are some of the fears and excuses that have kept you from getting well?

5. How will your life change when you seek healing in the areas of your biggest need? How will your kids' lives improve? List all the positive changes you can think of.

6. List a person or place that you will contact today (or as soon as possible) to ask for help. Write down the individual's or organization's name and phone number. When will you call or visit this contact? Ask a member of your Prayer Warrior Mom group or an accountability partner to hold you to your promise of getting help.

Learn to Love to Pray

Prayer should not be regarded as a duty which must be performed, but rather as a privilege to be enjoyed, a rare delight that is always revealing some new beauty.

—E. M. Bounds[1]

Falling in love with the Father means falling in love with prayer. Andrew Murray wrote, "Answered prayer is the interchange of love between the Father and his child."[2] We can't have fulfilling earthly relationships without love; the same is true about our prayer relationship with the Lord of the universe. The daily discipline of prayer gives birth to love, and the more we love God, the easier the daily discipline becomes.

I admit I used to think prayer was boring. God's taken me from "boring" to "roaring" through His Spirit. He will do the same for you! You can learn to love prayer by taking baby steps.

Dispense with the formalities and look at God again through the eyes of a child, with a pure heart and confident faith.

Maybe you grew up with a view of God as angry, violent, condemning, unapproving, or judgmental. You may have been taught that the only way to pray is by repeating memorized prayers that have little significance or relevance to your life. Maybe your father or mother was abusive, and you struggle to see God as good, loving, and kind.

If so, pray, "Lord, I've grown up with a false or incomplete picture of who You really are. Please help me see You as loving, righteous, and giving. Help me become a mother after Your own heart who reflects Your love and grace to my children."

Start today by creating a new prayer habit. Early believers often created "prayer closets" for themselves. Find a comfortable chair, a desk or table, or another place (public or private) that you can consider your "prayer closet." If you haven't already, purchase a pretty journal or a steno notebook for recording your prayer requests and praises. Pour yourself a cup of hot tea or coffee to enjoy as you sit down to read, highlight, and pray through this chapter and the scriptures at the end of it. If possible, also pray back through the scriptures at the end of every chapter and begin memorizing them.

You may also want to buy or make a plaque with phrases about prayer and put it in your "prayer spot" or a prominent place as a reminder. I found a darling plaque recently that says, "Prayer changes things!" I put it in the kitchen so I can see it soon after I wake up in the morning.

I'm an early bird, so for me, morning is the best time to pray. Morning prayer "rolls out the red carpet" for God, setting a tone of praise and thanksgiving for the day. It offers us a spiritual perspective that we can carry with us through the day. If we commune with God early in the morning and lay our burdens on Him then, we will be free to enjoy each day unencumbered, soaring on wings of freedom and joy.

I also believe that when our children see us praying for them early in the morning, God will engrave that positive image on their minds and hearts. I remember my own mother (who had six children) waking up at 4:45 every morning to spend at least an hour praying for us and for anyone else who needed it. She would faithfully pray through fat notebooks overflowing with prayer requests. Sometimes little slips of paper would fall out, and she would tuck them carefully back into her book so no request would be lost. God has seared that image in my memory.

When our kids see that we are devoted to praying for them, they will sense our love. Our example will warm their souls with a flame of peace and security. Ideally, it will also inspire them to become people of prayer themselves.

You may be a night owl. If so, don't fret! Your best prayer time might be in the afternoon or evening. The time of day really doesn't matter; all that matters is that you pray! Pray out loud; it will help you stay focused. Pray while you clean the house. Pray with your children at mealtimes. Offer thanks immediately whenever you receive a blessing or find out good news. Take your child's hand and pray with him or her when sad or painful events occur, or when you need direction. Let your kids observe your humble dependence on the Lord. Show them what it means to "pray without ceasing."

Your love for the process of prayer will grow as you learn to see God as your extravagant, generous, and gracious

Abba—your "Daddy." Think about how much you love your kids. Now, multiply that by a billion, and you have a smidgen of an idea of how much God loves you. Center your heart on the extravagant love of God for you through Christ. The Bible says that God is good, that He loves you fiercely, loyally, perfectly, and forever. He "rejoice[s] over you with singing" (Zeph. 3:17).

As your faith level increases, you will begin to agree with God about what is good and holy (and what is not) in your own life and the lives of your children. Your desires and attributes will begin to align with His. You will discover how to search out His will for yourself and your children. You will have peace as you learn to accept His "Yes," no matter how difficult that may be.

As you pray for your kids daily, your family members and friends will notice the difference in you. Your spiritual perspective will clarify and deepen like pure water drawn from an artesian well. I can promise that you will experience astonishing breakthroughs in your life and in the lives of your kids. It's not "magic"; it's the supernatural result of your prayers and your love-walk with the Lord. He says, "Call to Me, and I will answer you, and show you great and mighty things, which you do not know" (Jer. 33:3).

In Scripture, we see that Jesus always gave thanks, and His thanks preceded the miracles God chose to perform through Him. One author has written, *"Eucharisteo—*thanksgiving—*always precedes the miracle."*[3] You may need a miracle right now. The Bible is filled with them: the feeding of the five thousand. The resurrection of Lazarus. Jesus exchanging His life for us in a death so agonizing that a new word was coined to describe it: "excruciating." That's the most mind-boggling miracle of all—that God became a man, took our sins upon Himself, and died to redeem us. He chose to endure the cross "for the joy set before Him" (Heb. 12:2 NASB).

Prayer works; God promises us that in His Word. As you become a Prayer Warrior Mom, the Holy Spirit will bathe your spirit with increased faith, peace, joy, and trust. God will energize your prayers and use them as dynamite to blast through all the obstacles that are hindering you and your children from living joyful, healthy, and abundant lives. You will find hope and rest in God's everlasting covenant love (Phil. 4:7).

When you talk to God, talk to Him as you do with your best friend. Why do you enjoy talking to your friend so much? Why do you love spending time with her? When you call her, what types of conversations do you have? How does she encourage and uplift you? What do you appreciate about her? What kinds of fun activities do you enjoy together?

One key to all fulfilling relationships is *connection*. We love our spouses, family members, and friends because we share a deep connection with them. They're fun to be around. We have interests and personality traits in common. We may be in the same life stage. Our kids and theirs may be around the same age. Our shared connections make us "soul mates."

You and God can be soul mates too. You will learn to love to pray as you strengthen and savor the connection you have with Him. As you commune with the Lord more deeply, more often, your spiritual awareness will increase. You will "hear" the Holy Spirit guiding and leading you more clearly within your spirit. The flashbulbs of discernment and understanding will illuminate your mind as God reveals positive areas of growth in your kids' lives as well as problems, concerns, weaknesses, and spiritual issues.

Gardens that are cultivated and watered bring forth more fruit. The "garden" of your family works the same. To plant and cultivate a fruitful prayer life, we must depend completely on Jesus as the True Vine. He is the Vine; we are the branches. Unless we are rooted and grafted into His eternal life, *we have no life*. Life is Christ. Period.

Jesus said, "If you abide in Me, and My words abide in you, you will ask what you desire, and it shall be done for you" (John 15:7). *Abide* is drawn from the Greek verb *meno*, which means "to wait or remain; to live; to last; to stand."[4]

Jesus promises that our desires will be met *if we abide in Him* and *if His words* (God's Word) *live (abide) in us*. By cultivating a healthy prayer life, we become rooted in Him. By reading and memorizing God's Word, and by praying Scripture for our children, we create "living room" for God's truth to abide in us. The great preacher Charles Spurgeon said, *"If you want that splendid power in prayer, you must remain in loving, living, lasting, conscious, practical, abiding union with the Lord Jesus Christ."*[5]

What rewards will we reap for abiding in the True Vine? Jesus said, "These things I have spoken to you, that *My joy may remain in you*, and that *your joy may be full*" (John 15:11; emphasis added).

We gain a two-part blessing. First, Jesus gives us His joy, a joy that is perfect, mature, and permanent. Jesus had a joy that no one could snatch away from Him—not even the cruel Roman soldiers who flogged Him, mocked Him, and staked His wrists and feet to a cross. The Bible even says that "for the *joy* set before Him, He endured the cross" (Heb. 12:2 NASB; emphasis added).

Second, Jesus promised that when we abide in Him and follow His commands and the directives given to us in Scripture, our joy will be full (abundant). We will have joy and hope even amid the sleepless nights, carpool rides, mounds of dirty laundry, and emergency room trips. We will have contentment at times when we normally would have fretted, fussed, envied others, or complained about our situation.

God is the only Person with whom you can (and should) share your deepest self. I've discovered that much of the baggage and frustration of the daily grind of child rearing involves things that not even my own husband can understand. I have tried to communicate my feelings to him, but he can't always empathize with me. I share with him because I want him to know me and be able to partner with me in what I am going through. However, with his job and responsibilities for helping care for our children, he's weighed down with enough of a burden himself. He doesn't always know how to help encourage me and give my emotional energy a boost.

We want our husbands to inspire us, love us, compliment us, cheer for us, surprise us, and be "hopeless romantics." We're disappointed when they don't do those things. But I've had to accept the fact that my inner peace, my thought life, and my spiritual well-being cannot be based on what my husband does (or doesn't) do. You and I cannot expect our husbands to take the place of God in our lives. We can't expect them to love us perfectly. If we do, we'll be crushed with disappointment every time.

Instead, root your prayers in the foundation of Jesus Christ and the hope that He gives, which will never disappoint you. Teach your children to lean on Jesus for their emotional needs.

As you become a Prayer Warrior Mom, your relationship with God will blossom, sweeten, and deepen. Your confidence will grow as you enter into His presence more often and with more authority. Jesus said, "No longer do I call you servants, for a servant does not know what his master is doing; but I have called you friends" (John 15:15). As you learn to abide in Christ, you will discover the joy of becoming friends with God.

Today's Prayer

Heavenly Father, teach me to love my daily prayer time with You. Thank You for allowing me to experience the holy privilege of motherhood. I thank You today for each of my children: [State their names here]. Please help me to be a consistent and powerful example of prayer to them. Help me to teach them to pray and to depend fully on You for everything. Inspire me each day to be a faithful and effective prayer warrior. Show me a consistent time that I can use for prayer each day. Use my prayers as "dynamite" to destroy the obstacles Satan has put in my children's path.

Please reveal to me any areas in which my children may be struggling or suffering today. Give me wisdom about how to encourage and help them. Teach me to be kind, patient, and authentic with them. Thank You for blessing me with Your peace and joy today. I praise You for sending Jesus to the cross to redeem us from our sins. In Jesus' name, amen.

The Sword of the Spirit

I am persuaded that neither death nor life, nor angels nor principalities nor powers, nor things present nor things to come, nor height nor depth, nor any other created thing, shall be able to separate us from the love of God which is in Christ Jesus our Lord. (Rom. 8:38–39)

"Then you will call upon me and come and pray to me, and I will listen to you. You will seek me and find me when you search for me with all your heart." (Jer. 29:12–14 NIV)

> I wait for the LORD, my soul does wait,
> And in His word do I hope.
> My soul waits for the Lord
> More than the watchmen for the morning.
> (Ps. 130:5–6 NASB)

And Abraham believed God, and it was reckoned to him as righteousness, and he was called the friend of God. (James 2:23)

Small Group Discussion Questions

1. What emotions and attitudes have you typically attached to the practice of prayer? What was your early experience with prayer in your family or the church where you grew up?

2. What obstacles and misunderstandings have kept you from loving the process of prayer? Have you ever thought of prayer as boring? If so, why?

3. How would you describe your current prayer life?

4. Is morning, afternoon, or evening the best time for you to pray each day? What special details can you plan to make your prayer time more enjoyable? Write them down.

8

Be Persistent

The praying life is a life of diligence . . . Nothing
you give to Jesus is lost. Giving the thing you
love best to the One you love most is what brings
exuberant joy, the hallmark of the praying life.

—Jennifer Kennedy Dean[1]

Herbert Kaufman wrote, "The habit of persis-
tence is the habit of victory."[2] Jesus emphasized the critical
importance of persistence in a parable that reveals surprising
truths about our God and His extravagant generosity. This
story will transform the way you view God as your Father,
and as a result, He will infuse your prayer life with even
greater passion and boldness. Contained in the book of Luke,
this story is often called the "Parable of the Persistent Friend."

Jesus said to [His disciples], "Suppose you have a friend, and you go to him at midnight and say, 'Friend, lend me three loaves of bread; a friend of mine on a journey has come to me, and I have no food to offer him.' And suppose the one inside answers, 'Don't bother me. The door is already locked, and my children and I are in bed. I can't get up and give you anything.' I tell you, even though he will not get up and give you the bread because of friendship, yet because of your shameless audacity he will surely get up and give you as much as you need.

So I say to you: Ask and it will be given to you; seek and you will find; knock and the door will be opened to you. For everyone who asks receives; the one who seeks finds; and to the one who knocks, the door will be opened." (Luke 11:5–10 NIV)

As moms, we can cling to the promises in this passage: Ask, seek, and knock, and your prayers will be rewarded. Not *might* be rewarded. They *will* be rewarded.

This parable highlights the compassionate, generous nature of our heavenly Father. Do you approach Him as good, giving, and holy? Author and theologian A. W. Tozer said, "What comes into our minds when we think about God is the most important thing about us."[3] Another author says that even more important than what we think about God is *what He thinks about us*. You may not be sure yet whether you believe in God, but I can guarantee you this: He believes in you!

One author has highlighted some of the most powerful truths from the parable:

The requester cannot allow himself to become discouraged merely because his first or second request is denied. He must be persistent. The Greek word translated as "persistence" means "shameless," suggesting freedom from the bashfulness that would stop a person from asking a second time. Knocking once does not indicate perseverance, but "continued" knocking does.

God often answers us after long and persevering requests. He hears prayers and grants blessings long after they appear to be unanswered or withheld. He does not promise to give blessings immediately. He promises only that He will do it according to His will and plan. Although He promises to answer the prayer of the faithful, often He requires us to wait a long time to try our faith. He may allow us to persevere for months or years, until we are completely dependent on Him, until we see that there is no other way to receive the blessing, and until we are prepared to receive it. Sometimes, we are not ready to receive a blessing when we first ask. We may be too proud, or we may not comprehend our dependence upon Him. Maybe we would not value it, or the timing for it may simply be wrong. If what we ask for is good and accords with God's will, He will give it at the best time possible.[4]

Maybe you've turned to this book, nursing a broken heart because of a prodigal or wayward child. Maybe you've prayed for your adult son or daughter for years, but your prayers haven't seemed to make a difference. Or your children may still live at home, and you're concerned about their attitudes, habits, choices, and spiritual influences.

If so, please don't give up! God answers "continued knocking." I'm praying daily for you, my friend. As you and I keep praying and journeying together through this book, you'll collect even more strategies to help you intercede more powerfully, specifically, and effectively for your children. Stay faithful; even as you read these words, your prayers are ripping down spiritual barriers and strongholds in your kids' lives. If you need encouragement, please join our Prayer Warrior Mom network on my website at www .PrayerWarriorMom.com.

Now, let's look back at this parable to discover some prayer principles that we need to know as Prayer Warrior Moms. First of all, *we (as the ones asking for "bread") can confidently approach God as our friend, not as a stranger.* We have an intimate relationship with Him. Whether it's midnight, noon, or any time in between, we can lift our children's needs to Him and know that our prayers will be heard. Pour out your heart; He's listening.

Take a moment to think about your friends; which of them would you feel confident visiting unannounced at midnight to ask for something? Why would you choose that specific friend over another? Most likely it's because you have great faith in her giving heart and sacrificial attitude. In your time of need, you would only approach a person whom you know well, who loves you, and who will follow through with the answer to your request. That characterizes God too!

Second, *we are not asking for the bread for ourselves*; we're providing a meal for someone else. In our own lives, this may translate into our opportunity to intercede in prayer for an important need that has arisen in the lives of our children or someone else close to us.

Third, *the friend asking for bread is making a reasonable request.* He isn't asking for a new, high-fashion wardrobe, Louis Vuitton luggage, a lake house, or a sports car; he is asking God to meet a real need that he did not anticipate. Do your prayer requests focus on true needs, or just wants?

Fourth, *we keep asking with persistence.* Why do we keep asking, despite the fact that the "Friend" (representing God) initially responds: "Don't bother me. The door is already locked, and my children and I are in bed. I can't get up and give you anything"? We keep asking because we know He loves us; His very nature is love, and He cannot deny His own nature.

In Matthew 7:9–11, Jesus asked, "Which of you, if your son asks for bread, will give him a stone? Or if he asks for a fish, will give him a snake? If you, then, though you are evil, know how to give good gifts to your children, how much more will your Father in heaven give good gifts to those who ask him!" (NIV). God, because He is generous and holy, wants to give us good gifts. Matthew 5:48 says, "Your heavenly Father is perfect." He knows what's best for us and our children. Even though we may not always understand how He is working, He will answer our prayers perfectly, according to His own will and in His own time.

Fifth, *God will answer because of our "shameless audacity"— and because of His giving nature.* "Shameless audacity"—I love that phrase! Imprint it on your mind and heart. Shameless audacity means you pray big and you pray with perseverance. Shameless audacity means you aren't afraid to approach God with any request, trusting fully that He will give the best possible answer according to His holy will.

This parable is one of the most misunderstood in Scripture, which is why we rarely hear it preached in church on Sunday. Contrary to what some people believe, God is not a tyrant. The Bible says that His character is perfect, holy, good, and immutable, meaning that He cannot change. He doesn't "change His mind" or grow tired of hearing our requests. He doesn't say grudgingly, "Oh well. This lady has asked so many times that I'm sick of hearing her voice, so I guess I'll go ahead and give her what she wants."

God gives out of the generosity and the perfection of who He is. Psalm 50:10 says that He owns "the cattle on a thousand hills," so He has the power to give us anything we ask. The Bible also says that, at times, God "relents" because of His mercy when He hears our persistent prayers (Ex. 32:14; 2 Sam. 24:16). This means that He often grants grace in the place of judgment, and that He sometimes steps in to rescue us (and our kids) from bearing the full consequences of our sin. Psalm 106:45 says, "And for their sake He remembered His covenant, and relented according to the multitude of His mercies."

When we persevere in prayer with full faith, God often chooses to answer those prayers with a "Yes!" in keeping with His good and generous character, not contrary to it. Martin Luther said, "Prayer is not overcoming God's reluctance, but laying hold of His willingness." Our Father is "able to do immeasurably more than all we ask or imagine, according to his power that is at work within us" (Eph. 3:20 NIV).

Sixth, *God wants us to test Him, just as He tests us.* Lean hard on Him; you will discover that He is your immovable Rock.

Entrust your greatest treasure, your children, to Him. He will tenderly protect you and your "little lambs." Isaiah 40:11 says that God will "gently lead those who are with young."

Last, *we should follow the example of the giving Friend (God) in this parable.* When one of your children, friends, or family members needs your help, remember the compassionate nature of the Friend that Jesus described here. Even if the need is challenging and unexpected, seek to meet it. Embrace the opportunity to shower your loved one with compassion and grace. Remember that 90 percent of ministry is just showing up!

Trials and pain have accompanied the human experience since the fall of man in the garden of Eden. Even Jesus endured severe trials and "wilderness moments" during His life on earth. Hebrews 5:8 reminds us, "Although He was a Son, He learned obedience from the things which He suffered" (NASB). If you've been waiting, suffering, and praying for an answer for months, even years, and you have not received an answer yet, God may be teaching you the spiritual disciplines of perseverance, submission, and obedience. Stay persistent!

Friedrich Nietzsche wrote, "The essential thing 'in heaven and earth' is . . . that there should be a long obedience in the same direction; there thereby results, and has always resulted in the long run, something which has made life worth living."[5] Persistent prayer is "a long obedience in the same direction" that will create a clean heart in you and result in God's outpouring of blessings on your life.

Your heavenly Father has promised, "I will never leave you nor forsake you" (Heb. 13:5). And James 1:12 offers you this powerful promise: "Blessed is a man who perseveres under trial; for once he has been approved, he will receive the crown of life which the Lord has promised to those who love Him" (NASB). Keep persevering, and keep your eyes on the prize. Your crown is waiting for you.

Persistent prayer opens up a special communication line between your heart and the heart of God. I believe God's ear is specially attuned to a mother's heartfelt prayers for her children. As a parent Himself, He possesses a tender understanding of the compassion, adoration, and devotion we have for our kids. He created us in His image; He's the one who infused our hearts with that heartwarming "Mama's blend" of love that no one else can match.

My friend Kimberly has taught me some unforgettable lessons about persistent prayer. She and I met while attending the same MOPS (Mothers of Preschoolers) group at our home church. Kimberly learned to persevere in prayer as the Lord guided her on a harrowing spiritual odyssey involving severe financial hardship, her son Austin's illness, and her son Andrew's emotional struggles. Here's what Kim had to say about it:

> Andrew was two years old when Austin was born. When Austin was only a couple of weeks old, we awoke in the middle of the night and heard him gagging. My husband, Scott, ran and grabbed the aspirator bulb, shoved it down Austin's throat, and suctioned out strings and strings of mucus. This began our endless battle of dealing with Austin's sinus and respiratory problems.
>
> When Austin was about five weeks old, he began crying pretty much all day and most of the night. He could

eat only one or two ounces at a feeding, and he suffered from many episodes of such severe coughing that I was afraid he would stop breathing. I was terrified that one day I'd go into his room and he wouldn't be alive. I wanted to be the "miracle mommy" and be able to heal Austin. But I couldn't. I felt so helpless.

During this time period, Scott had the opportunity to become a partner in his architectural firm. We prayed about the offer and decided to accept it. We swallowed hard and wrote out that big check, expecting Scott to earn that money back quickly as soon as he became a partner in the firm. But instead, the economic recession of 2008 hit.

Around that time, I took Austin back to the doctor, and he gave me a can of new formula specially formulated for babies with severe stomach problems. It was only available by prescription from the pharmacy. I took the formula home, and we could tell a difference; Austin's crying was not as severe. So I went to the pharmacy to buy more formula. A small can was thirty-five dollars. A few weeks later the price went up to fifty-five dollars per can.

Scott's business continued to suffer. In order to continue paying their employees' salaries and benefits, Scott and the other partners had to reduce their own salaries. We were thankful that he still had a job, but every month's paycheck was smaller than the previous one.

After a few months, Scott brought home his paycheck, and it was only seven hundred dollars. He got paid twice a month, but still, fear and anguish flooded my soul. I knew that the cost of Austin's doctor bills, formula, and medications alone was much more than seven hundred dollars per month, and we also had a mortgage and other bills to pay. In addition, Scott was traveling all the time to help keep his business afloat. And Andrew was having trouble accepting Austin due to his nonstop crying.

I found myself in the situation described in Romans 8:26: I was so physically exhausted and emotionally weak that I didn't even know what to pray or how to pray it. The despair in my soul and the groans of my spirit were just too great. But I managed to come up with this desperate one-sentence prayer, and I prayed it over and over: *"Lord, please heal Austin, help Andrew, and provide for our family."* The sleep deprivation, financial strain, and stress of caring for two struggling babies became almost more than I could bear. I was barely hanging by a thread, trying to keep my family together.

Austin cried all night, every night. He woke up Andrew on many occasions. I grew angry with Scott because he was traveling all the time, leaving me all by myself with two crying babies. All I could do was pray and ask God to help our family. I kept repeating that simple prayer: *"Lord, please heal Austin, help Andrew, and provide for our family."*

As Austin's health condition worsened, Andrew began to struggle even more. He craved my attention, but most of it went to Austin. One day, I was driving the car; the boys were sitting in the back in their car seats. We hardly ever took Austin anywhere because he tended to scream throughout the entire trip. I looked in the rear-view mirror and saw Andrew lean over and start hitting baby Austin over and over in frustration. He was so tired of Austin's constant crying. My heart broke for both of them—and for myself.

As Christmastime neared, my heart felt heavy as I realized we had no money for gifts. One day, I went to the mailbox and found an envelope containing an anonymous cashier's check for four hundred dollars. We still don't know who gave us that gift, but we were so grateful.

After Christmas, Austin still was not doing well. In February, I made an appointment to take him to a pediatric gastroenterologist who attends our church. The doctor asked me what formula I had been feeding Austin. I told him.

"That's really expensive, isn't it?" he asked. I nodded.

He opened his sample cabinet, which contained stacks and stacks of cans of that particular formula. He called his nurse over. "Please take these cans and give them to Kim," he said.

"How many of them?" she asked.

"All of them," he replied. I gasped and literally sobbed with gratitude right there in the doctor's office. He gave me enough formula to fill two large plastic trash bags. That formula lasted us for several months. Words cannot even describe what a blessing that was. God's provision truly was a miracle. I knew that He had heard my persistent prayer: *"Lord, please heal Austin, help Andrew, and provide for our family."*

In the spring of 2010, Austin's sinus problems and ear infections grew worse, and he had to have surgery. In addition, my husband, Scott, had been ill, and we discovered that he needed to have sinus surgery as well.

I knew we were going to need help with our medical bills. My dad, who is a cotton farmer in west Texas, had told me to let him know if I ever needed help, but I had never had to ask for it. However, this time we were in such desperate straits that I called him. "Daddy, could you please send us a thousand dollars?" I choked out. It was heartbreaking for me to have to ask him for help.

A few days later I went to the mailbox and found a letter from my dad. A check for *five* thousand dollars fell out.

By this time we had been living on Scott's drastically reduced salary for *an entire year.* How was that even possible? The numbers didn't add up—how could we have paid our mortgage, all our other bills, and our medical expenses on fourteen hundred dollars a month when Austin's care alone cost more than that? But God had miraculously provided for our family every single month. So I eventually learned to trust Him and stop worrying about our finances. I let Him do the math!

When Austin was about fourteen months old, his health finally began to improve. Scott came home one evening from a business trip and said, "Wow! Austin seems like a completely different kid!" In addition, Scott's pay gradually began to increase as the economy recovered and his business improved.

When Austin was sixteen months old, he slept through the night for the first time. Hallelujah!

Now I can say that I am thankful every day for the two years of trouble that we went through. I learned that God is so faithful to answer when we are persistent in praying to Him. He answered all our prayers: He healed Austin, He helped Andrew, and He provided for all our family's needs. In addition, He gave me the strength to endure those challenging years, even when I felt like I had been pushed way past my breaking point.

Since then, I've discovered a new level of trust, peace, joy, and gratitude in my life. When I think back on the miraculous ways that God helped us during that time, my heart overflows with gratitude. Most of all, I have a renewed faith in my precious Lord. He is our provider and healer!

When I asked Kim what she learned through this experience, she said, "Don't dread the difficult times. Take them and say, 'Thank You, Lord, that You count me worthy to learn more about You through desperate situations.' Keep going to church and serving Him the best you can. And be sure to memorize Scripture ahead of time so you can cling to it during the difficult days."

In the section titled "The Sword of the Spirit" at the end of this chapter, I've included several of the passages that Kim prayed during her journey. Hide them in your heart; they will serve as an encouragement to you as you seek to be more persistent and perseverant in your own prayer life.

Today's Prayer

God, thank You for being my Creator, Provider, and Friend. Teach me to persevere and be persistent in prayer. Thank You for hearing me and being faithful to answer in Your own perfect time. Thank You for loving my children and giving me the compassion, wisdom, and patience I need to care for them each day.

Help me to be faithful in praying daily for my children: [list their names here]. Thank You for already knowing every one of their needs before we even ask. I ask You to provide for us in the following situations today: [list the situations]. I come to You in "shameless audacity," knowing that You love my kids and want them to love and follow You.

Thank You for Your compassion toward me and for relenting from allowing me and my children to face all the consequences of our sin. And thank You for answering my prayers when I approach You in faith. Every good and perfect gift is from You, Lord. You delight in giving good gifts to Your children. Help me to reflect Your kind, merciful, and generous nature to my children and everyone around me today.

God, thank You for giving me the heart of a mother, a heart that longs to bless and protect my children. I thank You for loving them even more than I do and for having a plan for them that is beyond even my wildest dreams.

Every day, continue to grant me a deep love for my children and a deep love for You. Help me to seek You first in everything, God. You promise that when I do, all the other things will be added to my life. You are so faithful to answer when we come before Your throne with persistence and faith. Give me the patience to wait for Your timing, even when I wish I could see the results of my prayers right away.

Like Kimberly, I sometimes don't know what to pray and how to pray it, but You know the desires of my heart. Give me wisdom in the following troubling situations, Father [list them now]. I leave them at the altar today. I thank You for hearing me and for having compassion on my children. You are the Good Shepherd, guiding me and my children gently beside the still waters. Thank You for having compassion on me and my children. Thank You for rewarding my persistence. In Jesus' name, amen.

The Sword of the Spirit

"For I know the plans I have for you," declares the Lord, "plans to prosper you and not to harm you, plans to give you hope and a future. Then you will call on me and come and pray to me, and I will listen to you. You will seek me and find me when you seek me with all your heart." (Jer. 29:11–13 NIV)

You need to persevere so that when you have done the will of God, you will receive what he has promised. (Heb. 10:36 NIV)

"Ask and it will be given to you; seek and you will find; knock and the door will be opened to you. For everyone who asks receives; the one who seeks finds; and to the one who knocks, the door will be opened." (Matt. 7:7–8 NIV)

Let perseverance finish its work so that you may be mature and complete, not lacking anything. (James 1:4 NIV)

> The Lord is like a father to his children,
> tender and compassionate to those who fear him.
> For he understands how weak we are;
> he remembers we are only dust. (Ps. 103:13–14 NLT)

I press on, that I may lay hold of that for which Christ Jesus has also laid hold of me. (Phil. 3:12)

"I will not forget you! See, I have engraved you on the palms of my hands." (Isa. 49:15–16 NIV)

Small Group Discussion Questions

1. What do you find most surprising about the parable of the persistent friend? What did you learn about the nature of God? How does this truth transform your prayers for your children, husband, and other family members?

2. In your group, discuss a time when you were persistent in prayer and saw God come through with an amazing answer. How did you change through this process? What did you learn about God from this period of waiting and praying?

3. Do you currently have the "shameless audacity" to bring your requests confidently before God? If not, what is preventing you? What changes do you think you need to make in your attitudes, your view of God, and your prayer life to be more faithful and persistent?

4. How did Kimberly's story impact you? Have you or a friend walked through a valley similar to Kim's? If so, what did you learn about God and yourself during this time?

5. How persistent have you been in prayer for your own children? At what times and in which situations do you tend to pray for your kids the most? The least?

6. What habits could you implement in order to become more persistent in prayer? These might include establishing a more consistent morning or evening quiet time; keeping a prayer notebook or journal; writing daily in your

gratitude journal; memorizing more Scripture; starting to take prayer walks, either alone or with a friend; praying Scripture more often; starting a prayer group at your church; praying with your kids every night before putting them to bed; and/or praying with your husband daily. Pair up with a partner in your group and hold each other accountable for implementing these steps.

9

Fast for Spiritual Breakthrough

*Fasting possesses great power. If
practiced with the right intention,
it makes one a friend of God.*

—Tertullian[1]

I like regular Coke. To me, there ain't nothin'
like the real thing, baby—even though I know nothing healthy
resides in that sweet, flavorful concoction of carbonated water
and high-fructose corn syrup. I swear that my SUV has a built-
in radar leading me straight to the nearest McDonald's, where
I can grab a Coke any time of the night or day.

Most of us gravitate toward our favorite comfort foods like moths to a lightbulb. Your weakness may be chocolate cake, ice cream, or Snickers bars. Maybe it's bread, pasta, or potatoes. David and I recently watched a documentary in which a woman ate dozens of boxes of ice cream bars every single day. After watching that, I never wanted to eat ice cream again!

Okay, maybe not *never*. But sad to say, our culture is so obsessed with food that the practice of fasting seems foreign to us.

First of all, let's establish that fasting is a spiritual practice, meaning that it's not about the food itself. It does help us curb our food cravings, but the goal of fasting is to help us develop a clearer, more focused prayer relationship with the Lord. Fasting combined with prayer offers incredible spiritual benefits, and it can also help us break the addiction we have to the sugar, fat, carbs, and flavor crystals in fast foods and processed goodies.

We've dispelled a common misconception about fasting; the spiritual discipline of fasting is not about the food itself. It's not a "diet" or a "cleanse" done simply for the physical benefits. It's not a "spiritual fad." It's not something that only "charismatic Christians" or "spiritual fanatics" do. According to the Bible, Jesus expected *all* believers to fast, as you'll see momentarily. Fasting is a power tool that we should wield with confident faith. I'll show you how!

My husband comes from a very conservative Christian background of devout believers in Romania. There, Christians often fasted and prayed. Several times when I was suffering from illness and intense stress during our engagement, my husband and his family fasted and prayed for me. I felt blessed and special when I knew that David was sacrificing his own food and comfort to intercede for me. He still fasts on Sundays as part of his worship to the Lord.

Biblical fasting is simply a decision to refrain from food for a set amount of time for a spiritual purpose. As Prayer Warrior Moms, we can fast in order to renew our spiritual intimacy with God, to seek wisdom about an important decision for our kids, to petition for healing and restoration for our children, or to gain another type of spiritual breakthrough or answer from God.

We tend to see fasting as optional, but Jesus didn't. He said, "When you fast, do not be like the hypocrites, with a sad countenance. For they disfigure their faces that they may appear to men to be fasting. Assuredly, I say to you, they have their reward. But you, when you fast, anoint your head and wash your face, so that you do not appear to men to be fasting, but to your Father who is in the secret place; and your Father who sees in secret will reward you openly" (Matt. 6:16–18).

Jesus assumed that we would fast as one of three primary disciplines of the Christian life outlined in Matthew 6: giving, praying, and fasting. He said, "*When* you give . . . *when* you pray, . . . [and] *whenever* you fast" (vv. 2, 5, 16 NASB; emphasis added). He taught us to engage in these disciplines out of love for God and other people, without fanfare. Our goal is to please God, not attain the attention of others.

The attitude of your heart when fasting is what God rewards, not the fact that you gave up Coke, pasta, or chocolate cake (or your food of choice). He acknowledges your sacrifice, but the sacrifice of a certain food is not "magic," as in, "If I give up chocolate for Lent, God will automatically give me everything I want." Fasting does encourage spiritual results, but more than that, it becomes a beautiful gesture of your humility, submission, and love for the Lord.

I've found that fasting can be an uplifting, rewarding, and joyful experience when I use that time to invest in my relationship with God. Fasting stills my heart and crystallizes the voice of God within my spirit so His will becomes evident.

At first, the idea of fasting can be intimidating and even scary, but fasting is not difficult, and you will discover that the spiritual breakthroughs are well worth the effort. In addition, your body and soul will feel lighter, freer, healthier, and more "tuned in" to the voice of the Holy Spirit. Fasting will eliminate your unhealthy food cravings and reset your taste buds so you can appreciate more natural foods. It will also retrain your body and your brain to be satisfied with smaller portions.

Jentezen Franklin explains one of the greatest benefits of fasting: "Your spirit becomes uncluttered by the things of this world and amazingly sensitive to the things of God. . . . Fasting is a secret source of power that is overlooked by many."[2]

Elmer Towns wrote, "Hearing from God is one of the best things that can happen to you during a fast. You stop listening to your body and catering to its desires so your soul can become quiet. Then you can listen to God only . . . Hearing God speak to you is different than listening to the six o-clock news. Unlike the TV, God doesn't speak if the hearer isn't listening."[3]

I recommend that you start slowly and simply with a short-term fast. Always check with your doctor before beginning any type of fast, especially if you have medical conditions. I do *not* recommend any type of fast for pregnant women or breastfeeding moms. Breastfeeding moms require a high caloric intake, more liquids, and a proper balance of carbs, fats, and protein in order to sustain breast milk.

The Bible describes three basic types of fasts:

- A liquids-only fast

    Only drink liquids. Some may choose to eliminate certain liquids, like coffee, tea, and soda. I've read of those who drink only water; others also drink juice and clear broth during liquid fasts. Others might include soup, protein shakes, juiced fruits and vegetables, or smoothies. There's no hard-and-fast rule.

- A partial fast

    Only drink liquids and eat some foods. You may decide to eliminate fast food and junk food from your diet. Or you may choose to eat all organic foods. Follow the leading of the Holy Spirit.

- An absolute fast

    This type of fast eliminates all food and drink (even water) for a period of time (usually not more than twenty-four hours; in a few cases, up to three days). The human body can become dehydrated very quickly, so I don't recommend this type of fast unless under the recommendation and supervision of your doctor.

You can choose to fast for any time period that seems help- ful to you. The Bible contains examples of varying lengths of fasts for different occasions.

LENGTH OF FAST	PEOPLE ENGAGING IN THE FAST	BIBLE REFERENCES
Half-day (12-hour) or Whole-day (24-hour) fast	Moses, Jesus and the disciples, Daniel, Esther, David, Anna, the Jewish people (during feasts and festivals), Paul, the prophets, and most of the major biblical figures	Deut. 9:9; Ezra 10:6; Est. 4:16; Jer. 36:6; and many more
Three-day fast	Jesus, Daniel, Jonah, Paul, Silas, Barnabas, Cornelius, and other followers of Christ	Acts 9:9; Acts 10:30
Seven-day fast	Samuel and the Israelite people, after the death of Saul and his sons	1 Sam. 31:13
Fourteen-day fast	Paul and other prisoners who were shipwrecked	Acts 27:33
Twenty-one-day fast (a "Daniel" fast; see the book *The Daniel Fast* by Susan Gregory)	Daniel	Dan. 1:16; 10:3

Thirty-day fast (one month)	The Israelites may have fasted for thirty days, mourning the deaths of Aaron and Moses; Jesus fasted for more than 30 days in the wilderness (40 days total)	Num. 20:29; Deut. 34:8; Matt. 4:2
Forty-day fast	Jesus	Matt. 4:2

Personally, I have not felt led by the Lord to fast for more than three days at a time. Maybe I will fast for longer periods when I no longer have young children at home. I believe God calls us to balance our commitment to fasting with wisdom about the amount of food and energy we need to keep our commitments to our husbands, children, and ministries. A God-ordained fast should boost our health and wellness, not jeopardize it. Preparation and gradual tapering off of food intake are required for long fasts, so please be sure to consult one of the following resources before you begin a lengthy fast:

- Dr. Donald Colbert, *Get Healthy Through Detox and Fasting*
- Kristen Feola, *The Ultimate Guide to the Daniel Fast*
- Jentezen Franklin, *The Fasting Edge*
- Susan Gregory, *The Daniel Fast*
- Lisa E. Nelson, *A Woman's Guide to Fasting*
- Elmer L. Towns, *The Beginner's Guide to Fasting; Fasting for Spiritual Breakthrough*

One wise man said, "Fasting of the body is food for the soul."[4] The discipline of fasting is like "spring cleaning" for your body and provides a surprising number of health benefits. Since the time of Hippocrates, many of the world's best doctors have touted the medical and health benefits of controlled fasts, in addition to the measurable spiritual benefits. Fasting helps regulate our body processes and eliminate toxins, especially when we drink plenty of water during the fasting period. When we reduce or eliminate our food intake, we should increase our liquid intake accordingly.

Author Lisa Nelson lists the following five reasons to fast:

1. Fasting helps us to grow spiritually and to overcome sin.
2. Fasting empowers our intercession and petitioning.
3. Fasting prepares us for spiritual warfare.
4. Fasting is an obedience to God's call.
5. Fasting is a response to a crisis in our lives.[5]

Fasting helps us eliminate the noise and busyness that clutters our minds and bodies. You may want to consider fasting as a family from other activities that may be interfering with your relationship with God.

I've found that our culture's obsession with technology can become toxic and all-consuming if we let it. (We tend to do a lot of mindless eating when we watch TV too.) The American Academy of Pediatrics recommends that for children over age two, we limit our kids' screen time to a total of two hours or less per day (including TV, computer, video games, etc.). The AAP does not recommend any TV or screen time at all for children under age two. A recent *New York Times* article states that, according to the AAP, "screen time provides no educational benefits for children under age 2 and leaves less room for activities that do, like interacting with other people and playing."[6]

In an article about the Mosaic generation (kids born between 1984 and 2002), author David Kinnaman stated: "A recent study by the Kaiser Family Foundation shows that the typical Mosaic spends 8 1/2 hours each day using various media, including television, radio, music, print resources, computers, the Internet, and video games. That time is compressed into about 6 1/2 hours since they often use more than one media at once (for example, listening to music and spending time online)."[7]

I also recently read a sobering article in *Parenting* magazine stating that the time we spend reading to our kids should be *twice* the amount of time they spend watching TV. Now, when I think about that, I try to reach over and grab a book to read to them rather than picking up the remote and flicking on the tube.

Do I let my kids watch TV? Sure. We try to limit their screen time to educational shows and videos (they love the LeapFrog DVDs), but fasting from TV would certainly do my family some good. How about yours?

Why was TV invented in the first place? Was it really for our entertainment? Was it for your kids' education? Was it so we could one day watch *American Idol*, *The Bachelor*, the news, or *Good Morning America*? No way. As a student at Purdue University, I remember my shock when I discovered that TV was invented for the purpose of *advertising*.

That's right. Ever wonder why companies like Honda, Chrysler, Pepsi, and Guinness have spent up to $20 million on a *single* TV advertisement? Because advertising works. By the 1930s, many Americans had stopped listening to the radio, and advertising revenue had dropped. So the Radio Corporation of America (RCA) purchased a license from inventor Philo Farnsworth in 1939 to begin developing his television system as a new means for advertising.

Fasting from TV and advertising could do us all some good, couldn't it? In fact, why not make a list of the three biggest "time drains" for you and abstain from them all for a week? You'll be astonished by the positive difference this makes in your prayer life, your marriage, and your relationship with your kids.

Here are some other reasons we should combine fasting (both physical and otherwise) with our prayers:

- Jesus taught it.
- Jesus and the early believers modeled it.
- Fasting amplifies our prayers and brings our bodies and minds into agreement with God.
- Fasting allows us to develop spiritual maturity and self-control.
- The Bible says that God will answer certain prayers only if we have fasted and prayed with full faith (Matt. 17:19–21; Mark 9:29).
- Fasting shows that we are serious about our love relationship with God.

Jesus linked fasting to our opportunity to "lay up" treasures for ourselves in heaven. He said, "Do not lay up for yourselves treasures on earth, where moth and rust destroy and where thieves break in and steal; but lay up for yourselves treasures in heaven, where neither moth nor rust destroys and where thieves do not break in and steal. For where your treasure is, there your heart will be also" (Matt. 6:19–21).

Let's say you need a crucial breakthrough today in some area of your life. Maybe your prodigal child has strayed far from the Lord. Maybe you face breast cancer or another illness. Perhaps your husband has been laid off and has not been able to find another job, or maybe your spouse chose to leave you. Maybe a friend has betrayed you, or you've had a hurtful experience in ministry.

Jesus emphasized that a period of intense fasting and prayer may be required before God begins to engineer your personal breakthrough in these areas. For example, Jesus' disciples once came to Him distraught because they had tried to cast out a demon from a man's son but were unable. They asked Him, "Why could we not cast it out?"

Jesus replied, "Because of your unbelief; for assuredly, I say to you, if you have faith as a mustard seed, you will say to this mountain, 'Move from here to there,' and it will move; and nothing will be impossible for you. *However, this kind does not go out except by prayer and fasting*" (Matt. 17:19–21; emphasis added).

Guess what, my beloved friends? *Moving mountains requires a lot of power.* You and I are going to have to step it up a notch if we're going to see God move mountains. We must pray and fast until our spirits mesh into complete agreement with the Holy Spirit of God. Then God will light the fuse and blow those mountains out of your way. He'll bring down the barriers and clear the obstacles from your child's life. Pray for Him to make the rough places smooth for you and your children (Isa. 40:4; Luke 3:5).

If you have problems in your marriage that are negatively affecting you and your children, consider this: Paul wrote, "Do not deprive one another [of sexual intimacy] except with consent for a time, *that you may give yourselves to fasting and prayer*; and come together again so that Satan does not tempt you because of your lack of self-control" (1 Cor. 7:5; emphasis added). Use fasting and prayer to re-create a sweet, refreshing spiritual atmosphere in your home and your marriage. Pray with your husband, if possible, pleading with the Lord to restore unity and provide healing in your marriage.

When you and your children have important decisions to make, especially those of a spiritual nature, apply the principles of prayer and fasting. The Bible contains the examples of many godly women, such as Esther, Hannah, and Anna, who fasted and saw extraordinary breakthroughs in their lives as a result of their submission to God.

My prayer for you today is that your name will be added to the list of Prayer Warrior Moms who saw God move mountains and do miracles in the lives of her children through the power combo of prayer and fasting.

Today's Prayer

Dear heavenly Father, thank You for offering us the privilege of fasting to deepen our communion with You. Please give me wisdom today about whether You are calling me to fast. I am concerned about the following issues with my children: [name specific issues]. I believe that through prayer and fasting, I will obtain Your wisdom about how best to deal with these issues. Lord, help me to fast with faith as I pray for every prodigal to return home, for You to seek and to save every lost child, for You to bless my children in every area of their being, and for You to shackle Satan and keep Him far from my kids. Use fasting and prayer to equip me to do battle on earth as the holy angels are doing battle against the powers and principalities of darkness.

Bless my children, [list their names here], today. Grant them physical, emotional, and spiritual wellness. Help me to be a good example to them and care for my body as Your "temple." Keep them from struggling with eating disorders or body-image issues. Help me and my children to seek You as our portion, the "food" that we need even more than physical food. Empower me to hear Your voice and gain assurance about Your will through fasting. Amplify my prayers for my children. Help me to emerge on the other side as a more victorious Prayer Warrior Mom and a stronger daughter of the King. In Jesus' name, amen.

The Sword of the Spirit

I have not departed from the commandment of His lips; I have treasured the words of His mouth more than my necessary food. (Job 23:12)

I beseech you therefore, brethren, by the mercies of God, that you present your bodies a living sacrifice, holy, acceptable to God, which is your reasonable service. (Rom. 12:1)

Oh, taste and see that the Lord is good; blessed is the man who trusts in Him! (Ps. 34:8)

"If My people who are called by My name will humble themselves, and pray and seek My face, and turn from their wicked ways, then I will hear from heaven, and will forgive their sin and heal their land." (2 Chron. 7:14)

Small Group Discussion Questions

1. When you hear the word *fasting*, what comes to mind? What past experiences and stereotypes have you had regarding the practice of fasting? What did you learn about fasting (if anything) in the churches you have attended? What was your family's stance on fasting as you were growing up?

2. If you were to begin a fast, what type of fast (and what duration) would you choose? Why?

3. Which of your personal prayer requests and concerns about your children do you think God might resolve as you practice fasting combined with fervent prayer?

4. Are your kids struggling with any persistent problems, such as destructive relationships, addictions, compulsions, eating disorders, body-image problems, a rebellious spirit, an attitude of disrespect, or other issues that you need to address through a period of sustained fasting and prayer? List the most critical problems. Would you be willing to fast for twenty-four hours and listen to what God has to say to you during that time? When could you start? Record the results in your prayer journal.

Hold Your Children
Loosely

It is one thing to show your child the way,
and a harder thing to then stand out of it.

—Robert Brault[1]

MOTHERHOOD REQUIRES US TO LET GO OF OUR KIDS AT many points along the way—and that process hurts. Your son looks anxiously to you for reassurance as he walks into his classroom on his first day of kindergarten, clutching his Batman lunchbox. Then you blink, and he's strutting across the stage to receive his high school diploma. Or your daughter plays dress-up in your 1990s prom dress, teetering in your teal satin high heels, and the next thing you know, Daddy is walking her down the aisle. What happened to all those years in between?

The letting-go process doesn't happen smoothly—we have to release our children in stages, and that's tough. Each stage jolts our hearts as we're forced to admit that our babies are growing up and becoming less dependent on us.

Our challenge as Prayer Warrior Moms comes down to one word: *entrust*. Instead of swooping in like "helicopter moms" to rescue our kids from difficult situations, we can open our hands and entrust our children to the perfect plan of our heavenly Father. This frees us from our tendency to control and manipulate, and it gives room for the Holy Spirit to soothe and comfort our anxious spirits with God's healing peace.

Entrust means "to give over something to another for care, protection, or performance."[2] The root of the word *entrust* is clear: *trust*. We can only *entrust* a person or thing to someone whom we fully *trust* to take good care of it. For example, when Jesus was suffering on the cross, He cried out in a loud voice, "Father, into your hands I *entrust* my spirit" (Luke 23:46 GW). He's our example of perfect trust.

The apostle Paul also used the word *entrust* several times in his letters to Timothy, his spiritual son in the faith. Paul wrote:

> I know whom I have believed and I am convinced that He is able to guard what I have entrusted to Him until that day. (2 Tim. 1:12 NASB)

> Guard the good deposit that was entrusted to you—guard it with the help of the Holy Spirit who lives in us. (2 Tim. 1:14 NIV)

Did you notice another term that appears in each of these verses? *Guard.* We entrust our children to the Lord, but we're also charged with the spiritual task of guarding them while they are in our care.

My friend Monique and her husband, Chris, have modeled courageous faith as they have dealt with the severe illness of two of their three children. Monique says:

My husband and I had been invited to wait in the doctor's private office, so we had an ominous sense that something was wrong. My mind reeled as Chris and I watched our four-year-old daughter, Allison, play with a toy on the floor. We sat there numbly, awaiting her diagnosis.

The doctor finally walked in. Slowly, he spoke these dreaded words: "Allison has cystic fibrosis. I'm sorry."

We nodded our heads, as if we understood what all that entailed. Of course we didn't, but we could see black storm clouds gathering on the horizon of our lives. Allison was admitted to the hospital for tests. The doctor gently informed me about my daughter's short life expectancy. Let me tell you, that shattered my heart as I realized how many of my hopes and dreams for my only baby girl would never be realized.

Allison's doctors deluged us with information. We needed time to grieve, but somehow, in the midst of this storm, we were expected to pay attention, comprehend, and practice everything the medical staff was telling us.

Then, just when we thought there was no way life could possibly get worse, the doctor delivered even worse news.

Our second son, Adam, had cystic fibrosis too.

Unimaginable. Our son too? Two lives cut short and ravished by disease? Lightning flashed, and the winds of grief tore at the fibers of our being. How could I stand it? Hadn't the first storm been bad enough?

After we heard Adam's diagnosis, I looked down at the white tile floor and felt a powerful urge to throw myself down on the floor and beat my head on that cold tile over and over until all this stopped. Forever.

Psalm 73:21–22 perfectly encapsulates how I felt that moment:

> When my heart was grieved
> and my spirit embittered,
> I was senseless and ignorant;
> I was a brute beast before you. (NIV)

Just then, I clearly heard God say: *"Only I can do this."* Verse 23 of Psalm 73 says, "Yet I am always with you; you hold me by my right hand" (NIV). I knew that the only way I could endure this pain would be by clinging to God's hand through it all. And when I didn't have the strength to cling to Him anymore, He would carry me.

During the storm of our children's illness, God gave me a special picture that I often sit back and review in my mind. In the scene, that storm is still raging and Christ is trudging through it—head down, wincing from the stinging rain, assailed by the wind. Right behind him is my husband, Chris, feeling nearly the same onslaught of the storm but clinging to Christ's robe. I'm behind Chris, holding tightly to him. I'm protected behind my strong leader and his Lord. Behind me is our oldest son, Anson. Holding my hand, he's concerned, but seeing that Mom and Dad are trusting in their Savior, he trusts as well.

Behind Anson is our second son, Adam. He holds his brother's hand and looks behind him, giggling at the antics of his sister, Allison. His other arm stretches back, holding her little hand. She'd rather let go completely as she reaches out to pick a beautiful flower in the sunshine. They know *nothing* of the storm.

When I bring this picture to mind, I know that Christ is leading us. He has power even over the storm.

The scripture that I've clung to throughout this journey is Psalm 73:28: "But as for me, it is good to be near God. I have made the Sovereign LORD my refuge; I will tell of all your deeds." God has truly been my Rock and my Refuge through the storm.

It hasn't been an easy journey. We've faced many challenges. The months following Adam and Allison's diagnosis were a very dark time for me.

But God . . . That's my answer for everything. But God *never* let me slip too far, *never* failed to catch me, *never* failed to comfort me through His people and primarily my "truth speaker"—my faithful husband, Chris. As the Lord promised, He was there, holding my hand through it all.

When Adam and Allison were first diagnosed with CF, some well-meaning friends and family members told me, "Wow! What a testimony your kids will have one day when God heals them!"

I nodded and smiled, but I knew that until then we

had three treatments a day, the chest percussion that we had to do ourselves three times a day, doctor visits, occasional hospital stays, and for me, the waves of depression that came and went. We needed healing *now*!

I understand now that healing can be both instantaneous and ongoing. Sometimes I tell my kids that they will live to be sixty-five (at least!), and they better get that through their heads! They smile and laugh, and we go on with our lives.

God showed me that, in a way, we *were* healed. Because of God's grace, death does not have its grip on our family. Our kids *live* with cystic fibrosis. They're not dying from it! And now that their faith is their own, they have that peace as well.

We know that more trials will come. We pray that they'll help our faith to grow and mature, and most of all, that they will bring glory to God.

As of this writing, Monique's three children are alive and well, serving the Lord. Allison is twenty-three and a history major in college. Adam is twenty-five and married to a beautiful young lady named Kensie. He is a high school youth director at my parents' church and also takes biblical studies courses online through Liberty University. Anson, the couple's oldest son (who does not have cystic fibrosis), serves as a staff sergeant in the U.S. Marine Corps. He and his wife, Rachel, have three children.

Monique's story reminds us of the fleeting treasure we've

been given—life on this earth with our children. We don't own our kids. We don't own anything, so we must hold all things loosely. All we can take with us is our personal, saving relationship with God through Jesus Christ. Our investment is in eternity, not here.

Author Randy Alcorn has written, "John D. Rockefeller was one of the wealthiest men who ever lived. After he died, someone asked his accountant, 'How much money did John D. leave?'

"'All of it,' the accountant replied."[3]

Psalm 127:3 proclaims that "sons are a heritage from the LORD, children a reward from Him" (NIV 1984). We have the privilege of loving and enjoying our kids, but our role as Prayer Warrior Moms is to dedicate them back to God.

We find a beautiful example of this type of surrender in the biblical story of Hannah and Samuel. Hannah was one of two wives of Elkanah. Unable to bear children, Hannah endured the cruel taunts of Peninnah, Elkanah's other wife, who had borne him several children.

One year, on her annual pilgrimage to the temple, Hannah made this vow to God: "O LORD of hosts, if You will indeed look on the affliction of Your maidservant and . . . will give Your maidservant a son, then I will give him to the LORD all the days of his life, and a razor shall never come on his head."

The priest, Eli, saw Hannah weeping and praying aloud. He mistakenly thought she was drunk. But she said, "No, my lord, I am a woman oppressed in spirit; I have drunk neither wine nor strong drink, but I have poured out my soul before the LORD" (1 Sam. 1:11, 15–16 NASB).

Eli then blessed Hannah and said, "Go in peace, and the

God of Israel grant your petition which you have asked of Him" (v. 17).

The Scriptures say that God "remembered" Hannah, and she conceived and bore a son. She named him Samuel, which means "asked of the Lord." Finally, God had granted the deepest desire of Hannah's heart: a son.

So what did Hannah do? She immediately dedicated Samuel back to God. When her little boy was only a few years old, she took him to Jerusalem to live and serve permanently in the temple. She kept her vow and entrusted her priceless treasure into God's care, as an act of thanksgiving for the gift of this son, Samuel.

Can you imagine waiting all those years for a son and then giving him up? What a heartbreak! But Hannah understood the spiritual principle of stewardship. She trusted that God had an extraordinary plan for Samuel, and Samuel became a great prophet and priest in Israel's history. He also enjoyed the privilege of anointing David as king.

As a Prayer Warrior Mom, you also can have the joy of releasing your children into the Lord's care and service. Here are some guidelines for surrendering your children to the Lord.

1. First, *remember not to put your children in first place in your life.* Our God, Yahweh, will refine us and toss into the fire anything that we choose to lift up and worship in the place of Him. I believe He will take us to task in any area in which we have created an idol. That includes the area of our children. Exodus 34:14 says, "Do not worship any other god,

for the LORD, whose name is Jealous, is a jealous God" (NIV). *Jealous* is a synonym for the word *zealous*. It means that God is consumed with righteous passion for His name and His people.

2. *Remember that this world is not your true home.* This earthly realm, which seems all too real to us at times, is just a tissue-thin veil and a shifting shadow compared to the rock-solid reality of our everlasting God and His kingdom. As Prayer Warrior Moms, we have the rare privilege of pulling aside the veil and peering into the Holy of Holies to see the spiritual reality behind all of our culture's smoke and mirrors. The only real power we have on this earth is the power of prayer. This world is a temporary dwelling place; our real home is in heaven with God. Our potent prayers for our kids connect them with the reality of God and His will for their lives.

3. *Release your children to God daily in prayer.* The apostle Paul wrote in Romans 12:1: "Therefore, I urge you, brothers and sisters, in view of God's mercy, to offer your bodies as a living sacrifice, holy and pleasing to God" (NIV). As Prayer Warrior Moms, we also offer our children up to God as living sacrifices.

When I was eight months pregnant with my son, my blood pressure started to rise, signaling the onset of pre-eclampsia. I had to be hospitalized and put on bed rest. That first evening I spent in the hospital was the most terrifying night of my life. I engaged in powerful intercessory prayer for my baby, fearing for my son's life—and my own. I reached a critical turning point when I found myself sobbing out this fervent prayer: "Lord, I don't care what happens to me; please just save my baby!"

That prayer indicates the radical shift that occurs in a mother's heart and spirit when she reaches the "point of exchange"—the threshold at which she values her child's life, health, and safety above her own. God reached this point when He chose to sacrifice His Son, Jesus, on the cross to save the rest of His beloved children—us.

God was faithful to protect and save my sweet son, Evan. The Sunday after Evan came home from the NICU, my mom, my sister Colleen, and my brother-in-law Daryl came to visit our family. In church that morning, we sang the song "Mighty to Save." Tears poured down my face as the full import of God's work in my life (and Evan's) crashed over me like the waves of the Pacific.

Ever since that morning, I've considered that worship song to be "Evan's song." I printed it out and put it up on the wall of his room as a reminder that God truly is mighty to save. I also saved a copy of it in Evan's baby book.

When my friend Amy Joy was pregnant with her fifth child, she and her husband, Layne, discovered that the baby had a metabolic disorder. Amy Joy's doctor warned the couple that most likely, the baby would not make it to full term, and even if she did, she would not be able to live outside the womb.

To help themselves grapple with the roller coaster of emotions they were experiencing (joy and loss, hope and despair, anticipation and anxiety), Amy Joy and Layne chose to start a blog called *Fearfully and Wonderfully Made*. On the site, they began to write about their experience as they awaited the birth of their sweet baby girl, whom they decided to name Maggie Faith.

Finally, at thirty-eight weeks, Amy Joy gave birth to Maggie Faith. After a blood transfusion and a myriad of other medical measures, Maggie Faith went to be with the Lord on March 16, 2010.

She lived for only four days.

Soon afterward, Amy Joy and Layne wrote:

Maggie Faith Olivo, deeply loved when there was only the promise of her, lovingly carried by her momma for 38 weeks, graced us with her presence for four beautiful days. Then she affectionately danced with her daddy into the arms of her Heavenly Father.

Our tiny, priceless pearl inspired us to greater faith in the One who taught us how to love and loves us more extravagantly than we can fathom.

Through their blog, Amy Joy and her husband have had the opportunity to touch the lives of thousands of other parents who have lost a child. Amy Joy wrote:

She was so beautiful and so fearfully and wonderfully made [Psalm 139:13–16]! God expanded my capacity to trust Him in this area. I remember the day I realized I really could ask Him to heal her of [illnesses] . . . The God we serve is so big, unfathomable really, and He delights when we pray asking Him to be Himself, to be HUGE [Psalm 77:13–14; Ephesians 3:20–21]. That realization was so essential when the findings from each test we had were worse news than the ones before.

I asked God for some pretty unbelievable things from a human perspective. I think He delighted that I would ask even when He answered me, "Beloved, I'm so sorry. I have something different in mind for her. But thank you for asking! Thank you for believing I *could* even if I *don't*!"[4]

My friend Tammy and I attended the celebration-of-life service for little Maggie Faith. Imagine my surprise when we sang the song "Mighty to Save"!

Again the flood of tears came. The words of the song caused a soul conflict for me, a deep ache in my heart. Mighty to save? Was it fair that God had answered my prayers and saved my baby, but He chose not to save my friend's baby?

Lord, why? I cried out silently from the deepest recesses of my heart. *Why didn't you save Maggie Faith too?*

I did save her.

The force of those words from the Lord almost made me fall over.

You did? my heart asked faintly. I had to ponder that for a while.

Oh. Yes. You see, sometimes my idea of what it means to "save" is not the same as God's idea. In His own perfect way, He did save Maggie Faith. He gave her family four precious days with her, which was more than they ever expected. According to God's timeline, that was just enough time.

The psalmist David lifted up this praise to the Lord: "Everything comes from you, and we have given you only what comes from your hand" (1 Chron. 29:14 NIV). David knew the pain of losing a child, too. In fact, he lost several. He understood that very few things are eternal; they include God, His Word, and our children. Instilling God's Word and His life-giving principles in our children is one of the most crucial eternal legacies we can give them. God says:

"So will My word be which goes forth from My mouth;
It will not return to Me empty,
Without accomplishing what I desire." (Isa. 55:11 NASB)

You are the vessel God uses to pass blessings down to your children and then back to Him again through praise. You offer a powerful testimony to the world when you purposefully entrust your children to our Father's plan.

Today's Prayer

Dear Lord, I thank You for having a plan for my children that is much greater than my own. I entrust them today into Your loving care. Help me to be there for my kids, but also to have the wisdom to allow them room to breathe, grow, and thrive. Keep me from trying to control or manipulate their lives. Show me Your will for them. Reveal to me their bents, and guide me in encouraging them to pursue the gifts You have given them.

Father, today I dedicate my children [state their names here] to You. I release them to You. All their days have been ordained and blessed by You. You understand the pain and struggles they will experience on earth. Give all of us the grace to bear them well. Guide my children in Your truth, Father. Keep them walking forever in Your ways. In Jesus' name, amen.

The Sword of the Spirit

Godliness actually is a means of great gain when accompanied by contentment. For we have brought nothing into the world, so we cannot take anything out of it either. (1 Tim. 6:6–7 NASB)

You are not your own. For you have been bought with a price: therefore glorify God in your body. (1 Cor. 6:19–20 NASB)

> For every beast of the forest is Mine,
> The cattle on a thousand hills. (Ps. 50:10 NASB)

> How precious is Your lovingkindness, O God!
> And the children of men take refuge in the shadow of
> Your wings. (Ps. 36:7 NASB)

Small Group Discussion Questions

1. List the names of your children, and next to each one, list three of that child's greatest strengths. (Below is a suggested template for your chart.) What gifts and abilities make each one special? What are some of your child's greatest interests? Discuss your answers in your group. Your group members may also have some excellent insights regarding your children's giftedness.

CHILD'S NAME	PERSONALITY STRENGTHS	GIFTS AND ABILITIES	INTERESTS

2. Now, take time to think about each of your children's weaknesses or struggles. In which areas would you like to see them grow and mature this year?

3. What spiritual goals would you like to see your children achieve over the next year? If you desire, write your answers down. Pray specifically for each child today in these areas. Ask the Lord to give you wisdom and a specific plan for helping each child develop and mature in these areas. If time allows, discuss these goals in your group and offer one another ideas for encouraging your children's growth.

II

Hear God's Voice Above the Noise of Daily Life

Make time for the quiet moments, as God whispers and the world is loud.

—Author Unknown

Sometimes we hear people say, "God told me such-and-such," and we secretly wonder, *How did you know that was God?*

Elizabeth Alves wrote, "'God spoke to me' is one of the most misunderstood phrases among His people; it can create misunderstanding, confusion, hurt, rejection, jealousy, pride and other negative responses. Perhaps you have run into someone who feels he or she has an edge on hearing from

God . . . If you are unfamiliar with the phrase 'God told me,' or you do not understand how to hear God's voice, you might feel inferior, thinking God never speaks to you."[1]

If you've never heard God speak to you through the Holy Spirit, don't worry. I believe you'll begin to discern the leading of the Holy Spirit as your prayer life becomes more active and powerful. You may hear the Spirit speak within your mind and heart as your communion with God deepens. The development of active listening skills and a quiet, expectant spirit are keys to hearing from the Lord.

As moms, we battle busyness and distractions as well as emotional stresses, such as exhaustion, depression, fear, anger, grief, and anxiety. Satan loves to ratchet up the emotional chaos in our lives to keep us from walking in fellowship with God. He jam-packs our days with noisy distractions in his efforts to get us to tune God out.

Why are we so addicted to activity and noise? Because we're afraid to be alone with our own thoughts. We're afraid of quiet and solitude. We avoid peaceful fellowship with our Savior because we fear that we might not be good enough without all our "stuff." We're afraid of what God might say to us or ask us to do if we sit still long enough to hear Him speak. We're not quite sure how to handle the sacred responsibility of being still and knowing that He is God (see Psalm 46:10).

At certain times in Scripture (especially in the Old Testament), God spoke clearly and audibly to His people. According to Job 40:6, God once spoke to Job out of a whirlwind. Habakkuk knew the sound of God speaking to him (Hab. 2:2). Elijah described the sound of God speaking as "a still small voice" in 1 Kings 19:12.

God has already spoken to us through natural revelation (His creation) and through special revelation (His Word). He may also choose to communicate with us at times through other methods, such as books, movies, videos, sermons, our conversations with other people, and our personal experiences.

When we've been faithfully praying for God's answer, we may hear that answer in the most unexpected way, at a spontaneous and surprising time. Sometimes God speaks to us in what seem to be the strangest and most chaotic moments. His "voice" (the voice of the Holy Spirit speaking within our hearts) cuts through the noise inside our souls as He makes His will and His message clear.

I've never heard God's voice audibly, but I've heard the Holy Spirit "speaking" within my heart. It's unmistakable. Elizabeth Alves has written that we hear God's voice in the "theater of the mind."[2] Hearing God's voice has happened to me most often when I was in the middle of a period of waiting, praying about an important issue in my life or the lives of my children, or transitioning from one life stage to the next.

For example, several years ago I began writing part-time for a company that specializes in search engine optimization (SEO). I enjoyed it but was not sure if the job was the Lord's will for me at that time. We needed the extra income, but I had a more-than-full docket with the demands of caring for my husband and two babies, maintaining our home, writing books, and ministering to my readers.

One day, I was playing with my daughter in our master bedroom when I heard the Lord say clearly: *"I'm going to meet this need in a different way."* I knew He was addressing our financial need.

From that day on, I felt a sense of peace as I waited to see what God had in store for our family. I continued to accept SEO assignments in the meantime, trusting the Lord to reveal His plan for my life. Several months later, my literary agent called me with the good news that this book had been accepted for publication by Thomas Nelson.

Recently, I took my son and daughter to play at McDonald's. Evan loves to scamper all over the place, clambering up onto the play equipment, speeding through the tunnels, and then racing down the curvy slide. At the edge of the play area is a tall, narrow gate with a lock on it. I'd never really noticed it before, but one day, Evan jumped up on the gate and exuberantly began shaking it. He threw his head back and let out a huge belly laugh as the door made a brassy *clang, clang* sound. I laughed at his delight; he's such a fun-loving and confident boy, and that brings great joy to my heart.

All of a sudden, the voice of the Holy Spirit rang through my mind loud and clear: *"He's going to rattle the gates."*

In astonishment, I looked at my son.

Then the Lord brought this passage to my mind: "On this rock I will build My church, and the gates of Hades shall not prevail against it" (Matt. 16:18).

Suddenly, my perspective shifted, and God allowed me to see my young son through fresh spiritual eyes. This little one has a powerful future in store! I believe that Evan will be involved in an influential ministry. Later, I told my husband that this insight from the Lord meant so much to me because I felt that He was giving me two assurances: (1) that my son would be involved in some type of powerful ministry; and (2) that my son would *live*.

When you have a fragile preemie, you spend so much energy, time, and effort hoping and praying that your child will simply live from one day to the next. You invest your entire being, just trying to help your child make it. After that truth spoken from the Lord, I've felt great peace in my spirit. I also feel an even greater responsibility to raise my children as powerful Christ followers and prayer warriors.

John 14:26 describes the Holy Spirit as our Comforter, Counselor, Helper, Guide, and Advocate before the Father. I like the New Living Translation of this verse, which says: "When the Father sends the Advocate as my representative— that is, the Holy Spirit—he will teach you everything and will remind you of everything I have told you."

In 1 Corinthians 3:16, Paul asks, "Do you not know that you are the temple of God . . . and that the Spirit of God dwells in you?" If you are a believer, you have the living, breathing, animate Spirit of God within you. As you quiet your soul and embrace the disciplines of prayer and solitude, you will hear Him speaking to you more clearly. The indwelling Holy Spirit will guide your own spirit and give you wisdom regarding your children. You'll stop fearing solitude and silence; in fact, you'll learn to embrace it.

Have you ever heard the saying, "Leap, and the net will appear"? Sometimes God asks us to step out boldly in faith and obedience, and then He reveals the next step we should take. My friend Jodi once reminded me, "God is rarely early, but He's *never* late!" By the time we need to take the next step, God will reveal what choice He wants us to make.

We know from Scripture that God not only hears us, but He also sees us in our distress. Here's a poignant example from Genesis 16.

God had promised Abraham and Sarah a son, an heir who would be the father of many nations. However, Abraham and Sarah got tired of waiting and chose to take matters into their own hands. Abraham had relations with Sarah's maid, Hagar, and Hagar conceived.

Immediately Sarah began to despise Hagar. She mistreated Hagar, and the maid fled to the wilderness.

The Bible says:

> Now the Angel of the LORD found her by a spring of water in the wilderness, by the spring on the way to Shur. And He said, "Hagar, Sarai's maid, where have you come from, and where are you going?"
>
> She said, "I am fleeing from the presence of my mistress Sarai."
>
> The Angel of the LORD said to her, "Return to your mistress, and submit yourself under her hand . . . I will multiply your descendants exceedingly, so that they shall not be counted for multitude . . .
>
> "Behold, you are with child,
>
> And you shall bear a son.
>
> You shall call his name Ishmael,
>
> Because the LORD has heard your affliction."
>
> Then she called the name of the LORD who spoke to her, You-Are-the-God-Who-Sees; for she said, "Have I also here seen Him who sees me?" (vv. 7–13).

In this passage, Hagar called God by the magnificent moniker El Roi, meaning "The God Who Sees." Everyone involved in Hagar's story suffered from Abraham and Sarah's disobedience. But God still had a plan for Hagar and her son, Ishmael. And from her story, we unearth the treasure of this powerful name, only mentioned once in the entire Bible. El Roi is the God who sees us and loves us anyway. He guides even those who disobey Him, and He protects those who end up as victims of others' disobedience. He has a loving plan for every mother and every child.

Just as Hagar's did, our hearts ignite with joy when we discover that we are hearing the voice of God our Father, who has heard our voice too. When He speaks to our hearts through the Holy Spirit, we know that He exists, He sees us, He loves us, and He cares about the intimate details of our lives.

Guess what else? The name Ishmael means "God hears." God's seeing is inseparably linked with His hearing. He sees your pain, and mine, and your children's. And He hears your voice, and mine, and the voices of your children.

God has bestowed on us the special gift of "mother's intuition." We know our children better than anyone else on earth knows them. So we can trust the Lord when He gives us that feeling that our kids are hiding something from us or battling a problem in the innermost part of their being.

Stormie Omartian shares the story of her young son Christopher, who was playing baseball at his friend Steven's house when the ball struck the front picture window. Steven's mother marched out the front door and demanded, "Who did this?"

"I didn't do it," said Steven.

"I didn't do it," said Christopher.

"Steven, you mean to tell me you did not strike the window with this ball?" she said.

"No, I didn't," answered Steven emphatically.

"Christopher, did you strike the window with the ball?"

"If you saw me do it, I did it. If you didn't see me do it, I didn't do it," Christopher answered in his most matter-of-fact voice.

"I didn't see you do it," she said.

"Then I didn't do it," he replied.

When Steven's mom told us what happened, we knew we needed to deal with this matter immediately so Christopher would not think he could get away with lying.

"Christopher, someone saw everything that happened. Would you like to tell us about it?" I said, wanting his full confession and a repentant heart.

He hung his head and said, "Okay, I did it."

We had a long talk about what the Word of God says about lying. "Satan is a liar," I told him. "All the evil he does begins with a lie. People who lie believe that lying will make things better for them. But actually, it does just the opposite. That's because telling a lie means you have aligned yourself with Satan. Every time you lie you give Satan a piece of your heart. The more lies you tell, the more you give place in your heart to Satan's lying spirit, until eventually you can't stop yourself from lying. The Bible says, 'Getting treasures by a lying tongue is the fleeting fantasy of those who seek death' (Proverbs 21:6). You may think you're getting something by lying, but all you're really doing is bringing death into your life."

. . . Quite some time after that incident, Christopher asked me who had seen him that day.

"It was God," I explained. "He saw you. I've always asked Him to reveal to me anything I need to know about you or your sister. He is the Spirit of Truth."

"Mom, that's not fair!" he said. After that, though, he always confessed any lies to me. "I thought I better tell you before you heard it from God," he would explain.[3]

Today, pray for the Lord to speak to you regarding His will for your life, marriage, and family. Ask Him, "Father, help me to hear the voice of the Holy Spirit. Deepen my wisdom and discernment regarding my own spiritual life, my marriage, and my relationship with my kids. Reveal to me any dishonesty or other issues that may be hurting my children. Teach me to listen carefully without being judgmental. Help me to extend grace to my kids."

Don't be afraid to lovingly intervene in your children's lives when necessary. Use the Scriptures to back up your words and actions. Let your kids know your expectations, and be sure to reassure them, "I love you, God loves you, and I think you're amazing!" God's purpose for accountability is always to bring about the restoration of our relationships with Him and others. He may be appointing you to help turn your children's hearts back toward Him.

Today's Prayer

Dear Lord, thank You for speaking to us through Your Word and through Your creation. We praise You for Your guidance. I pray that You will illuminate me and my children with Your spirit of truth. Give me discernment regarding my children's needs. When I see an issue or a problem, show me the best way to approach it. Flush out any spirits of negativity, deceit, or bitterness. Guard my children against harmful influences, misguided friends, and Satan's lies. Help me to be a godly and loving example to them. Teach me to confess my sin and ask for forgiveness when I fail. I pray that You will bring to light any problems in my children's lives that need to be dealt with. Make me and my children people of integrity and holiness. Set us apart and sanctify us for Your work, Lord. Keep all of us listening to Your voice and walking in the path of Your truth. In Jesus' name, amen.

The Sword of the Spirit

"My sheep hear My voice, and I know them, and they follow Me." (John 10:27)

"Behold, I stand at the door and knock. If anyone hears My voice and opens the door, I will come in to him and dine with him, and he with Me." (Rev. 3:20)

"However, when He, the Spirit of truth, has come, He will guide you into all truth; for He will not speak on His own authority, but whatever He hears He will speak; and He will tell you things to come." (John 14:26)

Small Group Discussion Questions

1. What misconceptions have you heard about God "speaking" to His people today? Why do you think this concept is confusing and controversial in our culture?

2. Have you ever heard the Lord (through the Holy Spirit) speaking to your mind and heart? If so, describe your experiences. How did they happen? What were the circumstances? What messages did God give you? Describe the outcome.

3. As you consider the ages, stages and situations of your children, how do you think the Holy Spirit is leading you to encourage and help them right now? Are there problem areas in which He may be calling you to speak up and provide accountability for one or more of your kids? If so, what are they?

4. What does it mean to you that God IS, that God SEES, and that God HEARS your prayers? How does this influence and transform your relationship with Him?

12

Be Your Children's Number One Advocate

Mother love is the fuel that enables a normal human being to do the impossible.

—MARION C. GARRETTY[1]

THE HAND THAT ROCKS THE CRADLE RULES THE WORLD."[2]

You won't find that proverb in the Bible, but it's true, isn't it? As a Prayer Warrior Mom, your presence and your words have more influence on your kids than anyone else's. You bear the privilege and responsibility of helping your children develop godly character, integrity, confidence, and a healthy self-concept. From birth, you "rule" your children's world.

As the person who spends the most time with your

children each day, you have the blessing of serving as their advocate and champion. You cultivate gratitude and grace in the seedbed of their hearts. You serve as their teacher, friend, example, confidante, playmate, comforter, and so much more.

Proverbs 25:11 says, "A word fitly spoken is like apples of gold." Nothing soothes a wounded heart like the tender embrace and the kind, encouraging words of a mom. I'm thirty-eight years old as I write this, and I often still need to spend time talking with my mama when I'm feeling discouraged. She and I live eight hundred miles apart, but I can always depend on her to encourage me, pray *for* me, pray *with* me, speak truth into my life, and just listen quietly to me when I really need to be heard. She's the ultimate example of a Prayer Warrior Mom—the one who inspired me to write this book.

Mom has always been my advocate, champion, and cheerleader. Since the day I was born, she made me believe that God had a special plan for my life and that He could use me to do something influential for the kingdom of God. Romans 8:31 asks, "If God is for us, who can be against us?" I believe that if we have praying moms who are interceding for us, nothing can stand against us—whether that opposition arises in the earthly or the spiritual realm.

I had a friend in seminary whose mother, Pam, is another incredible example of a Prayer Warrior Mom. Pam and her husband, Bob, served for many years as American missionaries in the Philippines. The couple had four children when Pam discovered that she was expecting again. Her fifth pregnancy was difficult from the start, with a great deal of pain and bleeding. A number of times, she was certain she had lost the baby. The couple made an appointment with a female doctor, who was supposedly the best doctor in their city to find out the options for saving Pam's life.

"An abortion is the only way to save your life," the doctor told Pam. "There's only a mass of fetal tissue—a tumor."

Pam and Bob walked out of the doctor's office, shocked and a bit numb, but resolute in their determination to keep the baby. The Lord filled Pam with an unexpected and indescribable peace that sustained her through the pain, bleeding, and uncertainty that occurred throughout the rest of her pregnancy.

Finally, in the delivery room at the Makati Medical Center in Manila, Pam gave birth to a baby boy, followed by an enormous blood clot that was even bigger than the baby.

The attending physician told the couple, "Your child is a miracle baby. I can't explain how it happened, but he beat all the odds. Only a small part of the placenta was attached, but it was just enough to keep your baby nourished all these months."

Before the baby's birth, his dad had prayed, "Father, if you want another preacher in this world, you give him to me." Bob had decided that he liked the name Timothy, and he hoped that the baby would be a boy. He told God, "You give me Timmy, and I will raise him to be a preacher."

Little Timmy grew up to become Tim Tebow, a record-setting football player for the University of Florida who went on to play in the NFL and became the first sophomore ever to win the Heisman Trophy. Tim openly shared his Christian testimony, and he gained additional media attention by wearing eye black that read "Phil. 4:13" and "John 3:16." As a result of his success, Tim Tebow has earned the opportunity to share the Christian message with thousands of people. God answered his dad's prayer: Timmy became a "preacher" after all.[3]

Tim's mother and father served as his advocates. They believed in the sanctity of life, and they stood up for their son when he could not stand up for himself. They hoped he would become a preacher, but they allowed him to follow the path carved out by his obvious skill and interests. They supported him 100 percent in the career he chose.

Abraham Lincoln, our country's sixteenth president, once said, "I remember my mother's prayers and they have always followed me. They have clung to me all my life."[4] I'm sure Tim Tebow would say the same today.

Before the birth of my own son, I felt the Lord impressing on my heart, "Marla, be *all there* for your kids." I obeyed His call by deciding that I would (as much as possible) be fully present with and for my children. I had been working part-time for a ministry but chose to become a stay-at-home mom after my son was born. Caring for Evan's needs turned out to be an around-the-clock responsibility anyway, so that worked out just fine!

You may have one or more children who have been labeled as "strong-willed" or "spirited." Maybe you have children who deal with ADD or ADHD. Perhaps they have special needs. If so, they need you to be their cheerleader. They need you to love, admire, and respect them, and they also need you to help others see them as you do: as beautiful, gifted, loved, and full of potential.

Labels can be soul-killers, both emotionally and physically. They make children feel bad, ashamed, hurt, and useless. And they wound parents, too, calling forth emotions of fear, confusion, resentment, shame, embarrassment, exhaustion, and anger. I'll never forget the time a church worker called my two-year-old son "aggressive." I was stunned. My sweet, exuberant, and fun-loving preemie, "aggressive"? Nothing awakens that "Mama Bear" instinct quicker than someone attacking her cubs!

However, I wanted to have a humble, teachable spirit. My son sometimes tossed his sippy cup on the floor or had trouble sharing toys; he may have displayed some aggressive *behavior*, but I knew that he was not aggressive *at heart*.

David and I partnered in prayer to help Evan work through his social and behavioral issues. He also began speech therapy with two incredible therapists. He loved it, and it helped him tremendously.

In addition, my husband and I began doing research to help Evan in his emotional and spiritual development. I read a book called *Raising Your Spirited Child* that was particularly insightful. The author wrote, "Spirited kids manage to garner an overabundance of awful, miserable, and poorly designed labels . . . Once an expectation is set, even if it isn't accurate, we tend to act in ways that are consistent with that expectation. Surprisingly often, the result is that the expectation, as if by magic, comes true. This is called the Pygmalion Effect and has been well documented by researchers."[5]

She continued, "It's easy to fall into the trap of labeling kids. Even if you tend to be an incredibly positive person, you might have gotten yourself caught in a swirl of negative labeling when it comes to dealing with your child. Starting today, you can choose to stop using words that project a negative image of your child."[6]

The author led a support group for parents of spirited children, many of them with special needs. In her group, she asked the parents to list the labels they (and others) had given to their children. They listed terms such as "argumentative," "unpredictable," "aggressive," "explosive," "demanding," and "picky." She then asked the parents to look over the list of "lousy labels" and discover the hidden potential and strengths in their child based on each of those terms. Here is how her group transformed their labels (and their attitudes toward their kids):

OLD NEGATIVE LABELS	NEW EXCITING LABELS
demanding	holds high standards
unpredictable	flexible, a creative problem solver
loud	enthusiastic and zestful
argumentative	opinionated, strongly committed to one's goals
stubborn	assertive, willing to persist in the face of obstacles
nosy	curious
wild	energetic
extreme	tenderhearted
inflexible	traditional

manipulative	charismatic
impatient	compelling
anxious	cautious
explosive	dramatic
picky	selective
whiny	analytical
distractible	perceptive

The author wrote, "Focusing on the positive labels may even allow you to recognize that your child really is the one you dreamed of having . . . As you pull your toddler out of the entertainment center, you can say, 'You really are curious. Let's see what you can discover over here in the kitchen cupboard instead.'"[7]

As I read and prayed about my son, I clearly heard God say, "Marla, reject those negative labels." Evan has always had a happy, exuberant personality. As I read about the nine characteristic temperament traits that most "strong-willed children" possess, I realized that the description did not fit Evan at all. (They are: negative persistence, high intensity, irregularity, distractibility, high energy and activity level, oversensitivity, low adaptability, high reactivity, and an often-cranky mood.) God flooded my soul with peace as I focused on helping my son develop self-control and godly behaviors without pigeonholing him with negative labels.

Many of the world's brightest and most influential people struggled to overcome negative labels, learning disorders, and other hindrances during their lives. Albert Einstein, Thomas Edison, and Winston Churchill were all labeled "dumb" by teachers in their early lives. What a tragedy! More recently, celebrities such as Salma Hayek, Keira Knightley, Will Smith, Jim Carrey, Justin Timberlake, and Ty Pennington have dealt with learning differences and ADHD.

If your child suffers from dyslexia, color blindness, or other visual reading disorders, he or she may benefit from the new ChromaGen eyeglass lenses.[8] According to a recent study, students using these lenses "went from seeing words hovering over the page, lines moving in waves, and words coming in and out of focus or appearing blurry" to seeing words that appeared normal, stood still on the page, and were easy to read and comprehend.[9]

When my mother was a single mom with five children, our family struggled financially. My dad had chosen to leave my mom for another woman, and we lived primarily on child support.

Mom said, "All I could do was pour out my heart in prayer for God to provide for the needs of our family. Then one day, the Lord told me, 'Dorothy, you take care of the children, and I'll take care of the rest.' And He did! God provided miraculously for our family, month after month."

One of my most treasured memories of my mom is that she was always *there* for us. Yes, she could have chosen to take a job outside the home. In fact, this often seemed like the only option that would provide for our financial needs. But she trusted God and stayed home, and the Lord proved Himself faithful by meeting every single one of our needs. Mom served as our advocate and champion. Whether we liked it or not, she always wanted to know:

> where we were going,
> who we were going with,
> what we were planning to do, and
> whose parents were going to be there.

Mom took responsibility for the care, protection, spiritual growth, and well-being of her children. She had high standards, but whenever I had a need or was dealing with an issue, I knew she would be there for me. And she still is.

I recently saw a quote that said, "Home is where your mom is." For me, that's still true. What a great goal for us to have as we become Prayer Warrior Moms ourselves—for our presence and our prayers to make *any place* "home" for our kids. Today, pray for the Lord to give you wisdom about specific, creative ways that you can be your kids' advocate and champion. Let them know you'll always be in their corner, cheering them on to victory.

Today's Prayer

Heavenly Father, thank You for being the One who is always there. You will never leave me or forsake my children. Be fully present for me and my children today. Help me to be my children's most powerful advocate and champion. Give me ways to show them that I am on their side and I will love them no matter what they do. Help me to buoy their spirits with positive, encouraging, life-giving words. Show me specific areas in which they need to be uplifted today. When they are in situations of conflict, give me wisdom to discern the truth about what has happened. Reveal to my kids that I am their cheerleader and that I want them to win the spiritual victory You have already orchestrated for them in the heavenly realms. Please reveal Your will for their lives, and help me to lead them in it. Give me wisdom about how I can specifically praise, encourage, inspire, and pray for each of my children today. In Jesus' name, amen.

The Sword of the Spirit

My little children, these things I write to you, so that you may not sin. And if anyone sins, we have an Advocate with the Father, Jesus Christ the righteous. (1 John 2:1)

You formed my inward parts;
You covered me in my mother's womb.
I will praise You, for I am fearfully and wonderfully made;
Marvelous are Your works,
And that my soul knows very well. (Ps. 139:13–14)

But now, thus says the LORD, who created you, O Jacob,
And He who formed you, O Israel:
"Fear not, for I have redeemed you;
I have called you by your name;
You are Mine." (Isa. 43:1)

If God is for us, who can be against us? He who did not spare His own Son, but delivered Him up for us all, how shall He not with Him also freely give us all things? . . . In all these things we are more than conquerors through Him who loved us. (Rom. 8:31–32, 37)

Small Group Discussion Questions

1. What is your response to the saying, "The hand that rocks the cradle rules the world"? Do you feel that this is true in your own family? Why or why not?

2. Describe some ways that you have served as your kids' advocate and champion in the past. Now describe a circumstance when you did not support your child the way you should have. What were the circumstances? What did you learn?

3. Were your own parents advocates and champions for you, or did you feel that they had a critical spirit? How has their attitude affected you? Did you have a mom who prayed for you? How does this influence your own prayers for your children?

4. Think about the labels that have been "stuck" to your kids. Are they negative or positive? Have you attributed negative or hurtful labels to your kids, either consciously or subconsciously? If so, what are they? Try the exercise described in the table contained in this chapter; list the negative labels and then transform them into positive labels.

Discern God's Will for Your Children

God's will is not an itinerary, but an attitude.

—ANDREW DHUSE[1]

WHAT'S THE ONE THING WE WANT TO KNOW ABOVE ALL else? We want to know what God's will is for ourselves and our kids.

Wouldn't our lives be so much easier if God would clearly spell out ahead of time which college majors, spouses, careers, ministries, and life paths our kids should choose so we wouldn't have to agonize over these choices?

The truth is, we *don't* have to agonize over them. God has a way of giving us just enough discernment and wisdom to handle the blessings and concerns that we face today. Jesus said, "So do not worry about tomorrow; for tomorrow will care for itself. Each day has enough trouble of its own" (Matt. 6:34 NASB).

As a mom, have you ever found yourself hoping or praying for something when you knew, deep down, that it was not God's plan? I know I have! Sometimes, we may pray that our children will not have to face the full consequences of their words and actions. We love them so much that we want to rescue them and protect them from pain. But sometimes we have to step back and let our kids learn life's lessons the hard way.

Hosea 4:6 says, "My people are destroyed from lack of knowledge." Knowing God's Word is the best way to discern God's will. As Prayer Warrior Moms, part of our call is to guard against worrying about things we can't control, hoping for things that contradict God's nature, and praying for results that are not in God's plan. We can be sure that God's will for our kids is never going to involve anything that directly contradicts His Word or His commands.

We can better understand God's will by distilling it into two basic categories. First, God executes His *active* (perfect and decreed) will. Romans 12:2 says, "Do not be conformed to this world, but be transformed by the renewing of your mind, so that you may prove what the will of God is, that which is good and acceptable and perfect" (NASB). God's will is stated in His Word. It cannot change; He has decreed it, and it will stand for eternity.

His active will is revealed through what He has already done (created the world, given us the Scriptures), what He will do in the future, and what He is doing right now (choosing to move in our lives and engage with His people through prayer). He carries out His plan in heaven and on earth through the power of the Holy Spirit in answer to our prayers.

His active will also contains the "discerned" or "directive" will, as we pray and discern the paths that God wants us and our children to follow.

Second, God executes His *permissive* will. He gives us and our children the option to choose whether we will follow Him. He wants us to love, obey, and trust Him, but He will not force us to do so. He will let us go down a sinful path if that's what we choose to do.

One author has written, "[His permissive will] encompasses what God allows, even though it is sin. God allowed Joseph's brothers to betray him, and to deceive their father, so that He might bring the Israelites (few in number) to Egypt, where God would spare them, and they would greatly multiply (Genesis 50:20). God allows man to reject the gospel, to willfully disobey His laws, to persecute the righteous, and so on. But in all this, God is still in control, and His purposes are being accomplished."[2]

God led my friend Jessica* and her family through a difficult move away from their home church and friends—and then the situation got worse! Jessica said,

> My husband's job provided an opportunity for us to move
> to a more rural area. We asked God to make it clear if
> we should go or stay. He answered our prayers when our

---

* Not her real name. Story used with permission.

house sold within three days of being on the market. We also knew that the new job would provide a better situation for my husband.

We planned to lease a house, but then my mother called with news of a house for sale that had EVERYTHING we wanted—five acres of land, a swimming pool, a wraparound porch, a red front door, and hiding places built behind closets for the boys to play in. We thought it was the place of our dreams.

Once we moved, however, I had a tough time adjusting. We loved the rural landscape, but the overall situation wasn't what I had thought it would be. I felt very isolated, as though our root system (all our friends and the church we loved) had been pulled out from under us.

During that time, I was comforted by the words of the song "Everlasting God" based on Isaiah 40:31: "Strength will rise as we wait upon the Lord." This continued to be my prayer every day, in everything—that my strength would increase as I waited for the Lord to take us back to our home.

One day, in a rant to my best friend on the phone, I said, "I wish this house would just burn down. Then we wouldn't have to worry about selling it, and we could move back home." Looking back, I realize now that the Lord had planted that seed in my mind to prepare me for what was to come. He did that even when my attitude wasn't what it should have been.

On the day after Christmas, we were in the middle of a visitor shift. My dad and sister had just left our home, and my in-laws and extended family were on their way to our house.

We had always been very disciplined about having our two boys sleep in their own rooms, so as to avoid bedtime issues. However, on that day, both boys were sick, so they were not napping upstairs in their rooms. Our younger son was awake downstairs in the living room, and our older son had a 104-degree fever, so we had let him sleep on the couch in our bedroom.

"Boom!" All of a sudden, we heard an explosion and the lights went out. My husband went to the garage to take a look. Already flames were billowing up the wall and curving onto the ceiling. We assumed that the fire had started from the electrical box, which was later confirmed.

"Call 9-1-1! Grab the boys!" he hollered at me. I called 9-1-1 and grabbed the two boys, my jacket, and my purse. Walking down to the road was quite a hike because we lived on a hill in the woods.

The boys had received a brand-new little Lab puppy for Christmas from Santa Claus. She was terrified by the fire, so she didn't follow us. We weren't able to chase her because we were trying to run away from the house as the windows began to explode.

I called our parents and family members to let them know what was going on. Finally, the ambulance and fire trucks arrived. Because of the strong wind, the firemen weren't able to immediately get to work on the house. They had to protect the neighborhood and saturate the ground surrounding our house. We took refuge in the ambulance and had the boys checked to be sure they were okay.

It was warm enough that day for us to stay outside, but once the second story of our home began to crash down onto the first story, I chose to stay inside the ambulance. I didn't want to see any more.

To be honest, I really didn't care about all the material things that we were losing. But I did pray for the safety of our new little puppy. And I tried to cheer up the boys. I told them, "Well, since our car just exploded in the garage, I guess we'll go ahead and get a minivan with automatic doors!"

Suddenly, we heard the radio crackle. A desperate mother had called 9-1-1 for assistance; her two-year-old son had stopped breathing in the middle of his afternoon nap.

In that moment, I felt the material world shift as God opened my eyes to the reality of our situation. Everything fell into place. My husband and I were safe. We were holding our two boys in our arms. And I realized that nothing else really mattered. I didn't care about anything else.

God's mighty arms of protection surrounded us that day. Even though He allowed our worldly possessions and family heirlooms to be burned and turned into ash, I knew that He was in control. And I knew that I wanted my family to be under His protection and guidance.

Once the fire was out, we were able to go up and see what remained. Not much—tons of ash and a few partial walls and a staircase. Our bedroom was still there, sort of. The firemen were able to pull out my husband's great-grandmother's antique china hutch with our china still intact. They found a Bible with the gilt edges blackened, a computer with most of our photos on it, and a framed scripture that said, "'For I know the plans I have for you,' declares the Lord, "... to give you a future and a hope ...'" (Jer. 29:11 NASB).

I knew when I saw that scripture, and afterward during the process of grieving and mourning the loss of our worldly possessions, that the Lord was going to protect us and keep us safe. He even brought our little puppy back to us—she had run over to a neighbor's house and waited at their back door to be rescued. We wept when the neighbor brought her back to us. We were so thankful for her life that it didn't matter that we didn't have our "things."

Of course, at times I still want and miss some of the material things that we lost in the fire. I want our home videos of the boys. I want the furniture heirlooms that were handed down to us through many generations. I want the hand-stitched quilts that my grandmothers and great-grandmother lovingly made for me.

Mostly, I longed to find something in the ash that both of my boys had used when they were babies. I told God, "Lord, I can let everything else go if You could please give me just one little thing—I don't care what it is—just *one* little thing that both of my babies used." We went back to the house and walked through the junk, looking for something.

Finally, I opened the shell of our dryer that sat on what used to be the back porch. Inside, I found a crib sheet that I had bought when I found out that I was pregnant with my firstborn son. That was a true miracle!

The Lord was so faithful to answer our prayers again and again. He made His presence known in both the little and the big things. Now our family clings to the following passage, knowing that He will always provide for us:

> When you pass through the waters, I will be with
>   you;
> And through the rivers, they shall not overflow you.
> When you walk through the fire, you shall not be
>   burned,
> Nor shall the flame scorch you.
> For I am the LORD your God,
> The Holy One of Israel, your Savior. (Isa. 43:2–3)

After the fire, Jessica and her family moved back to their hometown and rejoined their church and friends.

God, in His tender compassion, possesses a deeply personal love for us. He wants us to know Him. He chose to reveal Himself and His Word to us; we did not seek Him out. Romans 3:10–11 says,

> There is none righteous, no, not one;
> There is none who understands;
> There is none who seeks after God.

Sometimes we treat "God's will" as though it's the mysterious missing puzzle piece that could instantly make every aspect of our lives click into place. We chase it as if it were a tangible treasure that God has hidden from us like an Easter egg, and we have to spend the rest of our lives scrambling to find it. But we don't have to do that. We tend to think that once we discover God's will, our problems will end, we'll find the answers to all our questions, and we'll finally be able to live the "fairy tale." But that's not reality.

Sometimes, we even waste time and fail to do God's will today because we're so worried about figuring out what His will might be for us and our kids down the road.

Instead, claim and repeat this truth to yourself: "As I walk with God, He will reveal His will for me and my children at the right time." The more you study the Word of God, pray Scripture, and spend time with godly people, the more you'll discover that knowing God's will is not difficult at all. He never meant for it to be. Psalm 98:2 says, "The LORD has made known His salvation; *His righteousness He has revealed* in the sight of the nations" (emphasis added).

My rule of thumb is that if the Lord has not clearly revealed to me what my next action step should be, I wait and pray about it. I don't make a decision until the next step is clear. Rarely, circumstances demand that I make a choice before I feel that I have received direction from the Lord. In that case, I pray about it and discuss it with my husband, my mom, or another trusted friend. I also weigh the pros and cons of each option. Sometimes I write these down and pray about them, too.

Then I choose the option that I feel is the best and most pleasing to the Lord. During the decision-making process, I pray fervently for God to reveal to me whether this is the right door or the wrong one. As I begin to walk down one path, I pray for God to quickly shut the door and block off that path if that is not His will for me and my children.

James 1:5 says, "If any of you lacks wisdom, let him ask of God, who gives to all liberally and without reproach, and it will be given to him." As we and our kids approach each critical intersection of life, we must wait and pray until God switches on the red, yellow, or green light. He may give a clear "green light," a "go" signal. Or He may send you a "yellow light" signal, meaning, "Proceed with caution."

For example, your adult child may be interested in changing jobs but might not be certain whether to leave his current job. He may investigate various job options and interview for other positions while praying for God to either open doors or shut them. A yellow light may simply mean that God has not yet chosen to reveal His will for that situation, but He'll show you and your child what to do when the time is right. If no doors open, you can assume that staying put is the right option for the time being.

Sometimes God also grabs our attention with an obvious "red light," even in situations where we thought He was leading us in a different way. For example, my children attended the Sonshine School, an excellent preschool program at our church. At one point, because the program is only two days a week, I investigated other programs and prayed about a change. My husband and I felt that I might need more time to spend on my writing ministry. However, God closed all the other doors and made it clear that we were to keep our children where they were.

As a mother, you have a unique vantage point from which to determine your children's gifts and abilities. God's plan for their lives, their careers, and their spouses will often be linked to their innate gifts and personality. Look for their God-given bent, and encourage them in it.

Scott Adams, creator of the cartoon *Dilbert*, shares a story that demonstrates the transforming power of positive words. He wrote:

> When I was trying to become a syndicated cartoonist, I sent my portfolio to one cartoon editor after another—and received one rejection after another. One editor even called to suggest that I take art classes.
>
> Then Sarah Gillespie, an editor at United Media and one of the real experts in the field, called to offer me a contract. At first, I didn't believe her. I asked if I'd have to change my style, get a partner—or learn how to draw. But she believed that I was already good enough to be a nationally syndicated cartoonist.
>
> Her confidence in me completely changed my frame of reference: It altered how I thought about my own abilities. This may sound bizarre, but from the minute I got off the phone with her, I could draw better. You can see a marked improvement in the quality of the cartoons I drew after that conversation.[3]

As a mom, your encouragement can help your child "draw better." Your prayers, your belief in your child's gift-edness, can be enough to transform his or her perspective and even tangibly improve his or her technical and creative abilities.

Some of you, my readers, may have children who have turned away from the Lord. When our children become prodigals, one of the most difficult prayers to pray is, "God, do whatever it takes to save my son's [or daughter's] life. Do whatever it takes to bring him [or her] back to you. But please pour out your mercy and grace on my baby in the process. Bless my child. Protect him [or her]."

In his book *Beautiful Boy*, David Sheff poignantly recorded his journey through his son Nic's drug addiction to rocky road to recovery. Nic had once been a smart, funny, and well-liked young man, a varsity athlete and honor student who was adored by his younger brother and sister. But after he became addicted to drugs, he resorted to lying and stealing, his health deteriorated, and he ended up destitute, living on the streets.

During Nic's addiction and recovery, David and his wife, Karen, attended Al-Anon meetings. David wrote, "They say: 'Let go and let God.' And those three Cs that help even if I cannot always believe them: 'You didn't cause it, you can't control it, and you can't cure it.' But no matter what they say, part of me believes that it is my fault. People outside . . . can criticize me. They can blame me. Nic can. But nothing they can say or do is worse than what I do to myself every day . . . 'My son is gone,' I say. 'I don't know where he is.' I can't manage another word after that.

"Then, in a shaky voice, a woman tells us that her daughter is in jail for up to two years after a drug bust. She bursts into tears. But then she says: 'I'm happy. I know where she is. I know she's alive. Last year we were so excited that she was enrolled at Harvard. Now I'm relieved that she's in jail.' I think: So this is where we get . . . some of us come to a place where the good news is that our children are in jail."[4]

Pain, destructive sin patterns, bad habits, and addictions are not God's perfect will for us or our children. He does not (and cannot) commit evil; He does not *make* those things happen, but He *allows* them. He can use those hurtful habits to bring a wayward child (and that child's parents too) to the point of repentance. He can redeem even the most horrific situations. I've seen Him do it!

In a sermon, Pastor Tony Evans said, "You don't know that Jesus is all you need until Jesus is all you have." One of the most heartbreaking (but necessary) prayers a mom can pray is this: "Lord, let my son [or daughter] hit rock bottom so he will realize that he needs You. Send your holy angels to protect his life. Pour out Your mercy on him and bring him into a situation that will produce repentance. Restore him to me with wholeness and healing."

If you have young children, pray for God to reveal to you early on what path they should take in life. Pray for God to develop in each of them a heart that loves, obeys, and seeks after Him. Pray for each to maintain a teachable and accountable spirit. Every day, ask the Lord to keep your kids in the center of His perfect will and help them never to stray from it.

If your child has left the "sheepfold" and has gone astray, like the one wandering sheep who left the ninety-nine, pray for the Lord to guide your precious lost sheep back into the fold of His protection. Ask Him, "Lord, please pour out Your covenant love and tender compassion on me and my children." His Word promises, "The Lord is . . . not willing that any should perish but that all should come to repentance" (2 Peter 3:9).

Today's Prayer

Heavenly Father, thank You for being a God who has chosen to reveal Yourself to us. I praise You today for Your tender compassion on me and my children. Thank You for being trustworthy; I know I can trust You to reveal Your will to me in the right way and at the right time. Give me patience, and keep me from worrying about the things I cannot control or change. I pray that You will keep [name each child here] safe today. Keep them in the center of Your will. Help me discern the gifts and life paths that You have designed for them. Give me wisdom about how to teach and encourage them as they make important life decisions. Grant me the words to steer them back to the straight and narrow path if they start to go astray. Give them hearts that are quick to repent; give them the desire to return to doing what's right in Your eyes. Keep them from pursuing sinful passions that lead to death and destruction. Help me as I teach them to know Your Word and follow it. Do not allow them to be "destroyed for lack of knowledge." Through the power of the Holy Spirit, help me (and them) to discern Your will and walk in it every day with joy and obedience. In Jesus' name, amen.

The Sword of the Spirit

Do not be conformed to this world, but be transformed by the renewing of your mind, so that you may prove what the will of God is, that which is good and acceptable and perfect. (Rom. 12:2 NASB)

I delight to do Your will, O my God, and Your law is within my heart. (Ps. 40:8)

After you have suffered for a little while, the God of all grace, who called you to His eternal glory in Christ, will Himself perfect, confirm, strengthen and establish you. (1 Peter 5:10 NASB)

To them God willed to make known what are the riches of the glory of this mystery among the Gentiles: which is Christ in you, the hope of glory. (Col. 1:27)

Small Group Discussion Questions

1. Before you read this chapter, what was your understanding of the will of God? Did you think it was difficult to discover?

2. How do you think you would respond if someone were to ask you, "What is God's will for your life right now? For your husband's life [if you are married]? For each of your kids?"

3. In which areas do you feel that God is giving you green lights, yellow lights, or red lights today? What indicators have you received to show this?

4. How has the discussion of the active will and the permissive will of God helped you? What are the differences between the two? How does this influence your understanding of your children's relationships and walk with God?

5. Are you struggling with a son or daughter who is a prodigal or is walking far from the Lord? If so, how can you change your prayers for your child to reflect your understanding of God's active and permissive will? What do you think God could do that might bring about repentance, a changed heart, and a transformed lifestyle in your child? Pray for that today.

14

Live with a Spiritual Perspective

*A person who lives in faith must proceed
on incomplete evidence, trusting in advance
what will only make sense in reverse.*

—PHILIP YANCEY[1]

BEFORE DAVID AND I GOT MARRIED, I TAUGHT PIANO IN the Park Cities area of Dallas. One day, I stopped by OfficeMax to buy some office supplies and pick up some fun reward stickers for my piano students. At the checkout counter, the girl said, "Oh, you must be a teacher."

"I'm a piano teacher," I told her.

"You *are?*" she exclaimed. "With *those* stubby little fingers?"

I stared back at her, then down at my hands in surprise. Were my hands "stubby"? I'd never noticed. My mom had taught me to play the piano beginning at age five. Thank goodness she had never told me, "I'm sorry, sweetie; your fingers are just too stubby. You'll never be able to play the piano"!

As Prayer Warrior Moms, our positive and prayerful perspective on life helps our kids live in the light of kingdom reality. We help our kids establish their priorities and pursue their passions. If prayer is your passion, it will become theirs too.

Probably our best model of a person who prayed without ceasing (see 1 Thessalonians 5:17) and lived with a radically eternal perspective is the apostle Paul. He wrote, "For now we see in a mirror, dimly, but then face to face" and "For to me, to live is Christ, and to die is gain" (1 Cor. 13:12; Phil. 1:21). He lived each day with a hope anchored in heaven, not earth. To him, the pain and pleasures of this world were nothing compared with the joy of knowing Christ and "the power of His resurrection, and the fellowship of His sufferings" (Phil. 3:10).

Our goal as Prayer Warrior Moms is to show our kids that our hope is rooted and established in Christ. It is not based on anything in this world. Pain cannot tarnish it. People cannot steal it. Satan cannot destroy it. Physical death cannot affect it. Hebrews 6:19 says, "This hope we have as an anchor of the soul, both sure and steadfast, and which enters the Presence behind the veil."

My mother, Dorothy, has taught me extraordinary lessons about eternal faith and hope. Her firstborn son (my older brother, Jay) died at the age of four of complications from juvenile diabetes and a condition called Reye's syndrome. He died only a couple of weeks before my older sister, Deborah, was born.

My mom, who is the most faithful Prayer Warrior Mom I know, said, "Jay died on December 11, just before Christmas. We had already ordered his Christmas presents, including a cowboy hat and a pair of red leather cowboy boots. When we got home from the hospital, I went into the bedroom closet and saw those little boots. I collapsed to the floor and sobbed. No words could describe the despair that washed over me when I realized that my only son, my baby boy, would never get to wear those boots. My insides felt like a black pit."

She continued, "I was not a Christian at the time, and I didn't know the spiritual principle of hope. I didn't know how I could go on after that. But that situation led me to seek out God. I knew that I couldn't face life without Jay on my own."

"What did you learn through that experience?" I asked her.

She responded, "When trials touch my life, I know there's a reason. I may not know what the reason is, but God does. So I don't ask, 'Why?' I ask, 'How, Lord? How can I make it through this? What should be my first step?' He gives us hope even in the blackest night. He has a purpose for everything; He redeems every trial we face. I've learned to praise Him no matter what, because I know that He is faithful."

Originally, my mom and dad had planned to have only two children: Jay and my older sister, Deborah. But Jay's death gave my parents the desire to have more children. After his death, they had me, my brother Doug, my sister Colleen, and my sister Cecilia. Today, all of us are married and actively involved in church as well as other Christian ministries. God redeemed a seemingly terrible situation (my brother's death) and has used it to influence many lives for the sake of the gospel.

In addition, Jay's death has affected each of us, his siblings.

Although I never knew him, I think of him every day. Heaven has greater promise for me because I know that I will meet my big brother there. And I treasure the gifts of my son and daughter even more because I recognize that they could be taken away from me at any moment.

My understanding of God and my love for the Lord blossomed exponentially once I had children. For the first time, I realized that my parents love me no matter what I do. This transformed my view of God from fierce to forgiving. Growing up in a household with high expectations, I believed that I would be loved, admired, and praised as long as I did what I was supposed to: obeyed my parents, got straight As, didn't get into trouble, and so on.

After having kids, I realized that my parents loved me for who I was, not for what I did (or didn't do). And I grasped that they loved me because of who *they* were too. Their character made them love me, just as God's character causes Him to love us.

How about you? Is your home a place of grace or a performance arena? Do your kids know you love them whether they pass or fail, make the team or get cut? Do you encourage and comfort them when they face life's greatest disappointments—and even when they disappoint you? Today, pray, "Lord, help me to model grace and hope to my children. Provide me with tangible ways to show my unconditional love for them. Help me to be kind and supportive even when they make mistakes. Make me a mirror of Your love for them."

Breakthrough prayer requires you to radically shift your priorities. Satan-silencing prayer, the kind that rips down the devil's strongholds and illuminates the path of God's will for your child, requires time and energy. Snapping the chains of an earthly perspective may call for you to sacrifice extra sleep and other pleasures in order to get down to brass tacks with God.

Christian recording artist Steven Curtis Chapman and his wife, Mary Beth, experienced a shift in their spiritual perspective when their daughter Maria was struck by a car driven by their oldest son, Will.

Maria and her sisters had been playing in the backyard when Mary Beth heard terrified screams. She wrote:

"Mom!" Shaoey screamed. "Will hit Maria with the car!"

I ran down the few steps to the garage and rounded the corner toward the driveway. Will was holding Maria, crying and pleading for her to wake up. Both of them were covered in blood.

"Call 911!" I yelled. "Get your dad!"

I took Maria from Will. She was limp, like she was asleep . . . There was a puddle of blood about four feet in diameter on the driveway. Blood was streaming from her ears, her nose, her mouth. I tried to clear as much of it from her mouth as possible and started rescue breathing. But she wasn't responding.

Will was in shock. He couldn't dial 911.

Steven came around the back corner of the house and saw me covered in blood . . . "Will hit her with the car!" I cried. He took over the rescue breathing while I ran into the kitchen and called 911 on the home phone.

"The first thing you need to do is dispatch LifeFlight!" I screamed. "My little girl has been hit by a car and it's really bad . . . My husband's working on her . . . This is a trauma situation and we *will* need LifeFlight. Please, believe me, get LifeFlight here! Help me, oh my God, please help me!"

The ambulance arrived. They loaded Maria onto a stretcher while continuing to work on her. The LifeFlight helicopter landed in a neighbor's field down the street.

As we followed the ambulance down the driveway, Steven yelled at the top of his voice, "Will Franklin! Just remember, your father loves you!"[2]

A friend drove the Chapmans to Vanderbilt Hospital in Nashville, following the LifeFlight helicopter with Maria on board. Rush-hour traffic slowed to an unbearable crawl. When Steven and Mary Beth finally reached the ER, Mary Beth saw a friend curled up in a ball on the floor, sobbing. As she and Steven walked through the ER, many of their family and friends were standing there, looking at them with stricken faces. A hospital staff person walked up to them and calmly said, "You need to come this way, with me."

Mary Beth screamed, "No! No! I don't want to go that way! Please, no!"

The doctors and nurses took the Chapmans to a small room beyond the ER, where they said that while they had done everything they could, Maria had, in fact, died. They eventually allowed the Chapmans into the trauma room, where Maria was lying as if she were asleep. The only mark on her was a small abrasion on the side of her forehead.

"Oh, God!" Steven cried. "Breathe life into Maria! Please bring her back to life!" He knew God could do that if He chose to.

Mary Beth knew that too. But she also knew that God had healed Maria in a way they didn't want. "We've got to let her go, sweetie," she whispered. "It's time to let her go."

Mary Beth wrote,

Somehow in that unthinkable moment it became clear to Steven and me that we were standing at the very door of heaven, placing our little girl carefully in the arms of Jesus, desperately trusting that she would be safe there until we could come and join her.

I heard Steven's voice explaining to those in the room that this was an eternal moment. "The only thing I can say to honor the life of my little girl and our terrible loss at this moment is to ask you, please don't miss this . . . We will all stand here one day and face eternity. If you don't know the One who can give you eternal life, His name is Jesus . . . You need to meet Him and you really need to meet my little girl in heaven . . . she's amazing."

Steven and I bent over and kissed Maria's forehead. I stroked her face and tucked her hair back behind her ear one last time. Then we walked out to meet our friends and begin our long journey of grieving and waiting until we would pass through heaven's door ourselves.[3]

About three months after Maria's death, the Chapmans gave their first live TV interview about the incident on *Good Morning America*. Their extraordinary testimony and their choice to praise God even in the face of their devastating loss have given hope to thousands of people, prompting many to embrace the gospel. The Lord used their faithfulness in the face of intense grief and pain to usher thousands of people into His eternal kingdom.

God sees your pain and the personal struggles you have with your own children. Come to Him with open arms and let Him transform your trials into triumph. Paul wrote in 1 Thessalonians 4:13, "We do not want you to be uninformed, brethren, about those who are asleep, so that you will not grieve as do the rest who have no hope" (NASB). Even in your grief, *you always have hope* through the power of Christ and His resurrection.

Today's Prayer

Heavenly Father, keeping a spiritual perspective on this earth is one of the toughest things we could ever do. Please keep me from drowning in my problems and doubts. Help me remain anchored in You. I choose to look to Christ as my eternal hope, the One who is seated in the heavenly places. Hold tight to me and my children. Allow me to be a buoy for them during stormy times. Keep all of us from sinking. Help me be a vision-caster for my kids, always helping them see beyond the limits of their finite circumstances. Help me see and appreciate the best in them and others. Help all of us realize that the pain and pleasure of this world are temporary. Keep us focused on the hope that does not disappoint. Thank You for allowing us to grieve with hope. In Jesus' name, amen.

The Sword of the Spirit

Let us hold fast the confession of our hope without wavering, for He who promised is faithful; and let us consider how to stimulate one another to love and good deeds, not forsaking our own assembling together, as is the habit of some, but encouraging one another; and all the more as you see the day drawing near. (Heb. 10:23–25 NASB)

But whatever things were gain to me, those things I have counted as loss for the sake of Christ. More than that, I count all things to be loss in view of the surpassing value of knowing Christ Jesus my Lord, for whom I have suffered the loss of all things, and count them but rubbish so that I may gain Christ, and may be found in Him. (Phil. 3:7–9 NASB)

We also exult in our tribulations, knowing that tribulation brings about perseverance; and perseverance, proven character; and proven character, hope; and hope does not disappoint, because the love of God has been poured out within our hearts through the Holy Spirit who was given to us. (Rom. 5:3–5)

Small Group Discussion Questions

1. What is the greatest loss you have ever experienced? How did it affect you as a mother? Now, when you look back, can you see any good things that have resulted from that experience? If so, what are they? How have you changed as a result of your loss?

2. How has motherhood transformed your view of your parents? How has it changed and expanded your view of God?

3. In what situations might God be asking you today to "trust in advance what will only make sense in reverse"?

4. Do you take joy and pride in your role as a mom? To you, what are the greatest blessings of motherhood?

5. If you knew that you only had a few days left with each of your children, what activities would you do with them? What would you say to them? How would you demonstrate to them how much you love, treasure, and cherish them? Now, go and do all those things!

Model Forgiveness
and Grace

*To forgive is to set a prisoner free and
discover that the prisoner was you.*

—Lewis Smedes[1]

During a British conference on comparative religions, experts
from around the world debated what belief, if any, was unique
to the Christian faith. They began eliminating possibilities.
Incarnation? Other religions had different versions of gods'
appearing in human form. Resurrection? Again, other religions had accounts of return from death. The debate went on
for some time until C. S. Lewis wandered into the room.

"What's the rumpus about?" he asked.

One of the men told Lewis that his colleagues were discussing Christianity's unique contribution among world religions.

Lewis responded, "Oh, that's easy. It's grace."[2]

Only God offers us grace instead of condemnation. Only God has provided a way for Our Mediator, Jesus Christ, to forgive our sin when we deserve judgment. He tossed us the lifeline of prayer so we could live in communion with Him.

Did you realize that *only Christianity* offers faith-based salvation established on the finished work of Jesus Christ? By rising from the dead, Jesus broke the curse of sin and death. Ephesians 2:8–9 says, "For by grace you have been saved through faith, and that not of yourselves; it is the gift of God, not of works, lest anyone should boast." Our good works do not "earn" us salvation, eternal life, or a place in heaven. Only our acceptance of God's grace and salvation through Jesus Christ can do that.

All other religious systems are based on works; they can't offer any assurance of salvation. In other world religions, you can never be sure if you have done enough good works to "cancel out" your sin or your bad deeds. As a result, you can never be sure if you are saved or not. Some of these systems use fear, guilt, shame, and lack of knowledge to scare and manipulate people into obeying their religious rules. In these systems, the concept of grace is nowhere to be found.

When Jesus died on the cross and rose from the dead, He snapped the shackles imposed by every graceless religious system. And because our God is a God of forgiveness and grace, we can be moms of grace.

In order to bless our kids and model Christlikeness to them, we can cultivate a grace-based atmosphere in our homes. We can offer grace-based consequences in the place of harsh condemnation. The Pharisees, elders, and scribes loved to grant Jesus the opportunity to condemn people, but He didn't. When a repentant sinner entered into the presence of Jesus, that was a "grace place."

How much effort are you putting into making your home a "grace place" for your kids?

I'll admit that offering grace is not always fun or easy. Being "fair," offering judgment, condemning others for their faults, and clinging to grudges can be much easier than gifting others with the blessing of forgiveness.

The English poet Alexander Pope wrote, "To err is human; to forgive, divine."[3] Because we're flawed humans, grace and forgiveness don't flow naturally from our fleshly spirits. These attributes are divine gifts, showered upon us like a refreshing spring rain from the Author of life.

For me, on most days, grace looks like patience. It's offering a loving gesture and a kind word to my kids when I feel like yelling instead. It's scrubbing mashed banana and cereal bars out of the carpet—again—without harping, "How many times do I have to tell you not to eat in the living room?" My friend Caryn said that she prays throughout the day, "God, be my patience." Now I often find myself praying that too.

We can offer grace and forgiveness to our children because *we've been offered grace and forgiveness*. We love them because *God first loved us*. First John 4:10 says, "In this is love, not that we loved God, but that He loved us and sent His Son to be the propitiation for our sins."

One of the ways we can offer grace to our children is by thinking—and speaking—rightly about them and the parenting challenges that we face. As Prayer Warrior Moms, we can take every thought (and word) "captive to the obedience of Christ," knowing that the struggles of this life will not last forever (2 Cor. 10:5 NASB).

In her excellent book *52 Things Kids Need from a Mom*, author Angela Thomas offers several fun and practical tips for making your home a place of grace and forgiveness. Here are some of them:

- Let your kids see you praying every day. Even better, let them join you.
- Be sure to touch each of your children every day—a brush on the shoulder, a hug, a pat on the back before school, a kiss good night.
- Give specific compliments and praise.
- Prioritize sitting down together for dinner as a family.
- Set boundaries and be consistent about discipline. Play the "MOM" card (say no) when you have to.
- Keep your promises. If your plans change, communicate that to your children.
- Involve your children in giving to people who are less fortunate than your family.
- Choose your battles; don't point out every one of your children's flaws. Miss a few things they do wrong. Exhibit the character of Christ and allow room for grace. Be a peacemaker instead of a perfectionist.
- Occasionally be a "supermom" and go all out for them. Plan a special surprise, a big birthday party, or something else over-the-top to communicate to them, "I think you're awesome!"

- Talk to them and listen to them as though they are fascinating people; they are!
- Make a big deal out of God. Show them that God is number one in your house. Be "doers of the Word and not hearers only" (James 1:22).
- Let them make dumb mistakes without condemnation.
- Introduce them to your best friend, Jesus.[4]

More than anything else in this world, our children need grace. I believe that when our sons and daughters look back over the arc of their lives, their relationships with us will be influenced most by this: whether we were moms who modeled grace instead of grudges.

As I have traveled and spoken over the years, I've had the privilege of meeting many beloved women (me included) who were hurt by their distant, disconnected, or abusive fathers. Those wounds strike deep, and working through them is not easy.

But moms who have had critical, nagging, or abusive *mothers* seem to struggle even more. The pain of having a breach in the fundamental mother-child relationship can be almost unbearable without the healing power of God through the Holy Spirit. Usually, resolving these issues requires years of wise Christian counseling and prayer. If you need help, please reach out to a Christian counselor in your area. Being a healthy mom requires you to resolve any lingering issues you may have with your own parents.

In Isaiah 58, our heavenly Father describes the amazing results we reap when we choose to offer grace and forgiveness to our kids and to those who have hurt us. When we forgive, we "loose the bonds of wickedness, . . . undo the heavy burdens, . . . let the oppressed go free, and . . . break every yoke" (v. 6).

What could happen in your life today if you chose to release those burdens of bitterness? God says:

> "Then your light shall break forth like the morning,
> Your healing shall spring forth speedily,
> And your righteousness shall go before you;
> The glory of the LORD shall be your rear guard.
> Then you shall call, and the LORD will answer;
> You shall cry, and He will say, 'Here I am.' . . .
> You shall raise up the foundations of many
>   generations;
> And you shall be called the Repairer of the Breach,
> The Restorer of Streets to Dwell In." (Isa. 58:8–9, 12)

I want to be called a "Repairer of the Breach," don't you?

In his book *Not a Fan*, Kyle Idleman has offered a powerful illustration of grace. He wrote:

> My wife bought a white loveseat to go in the room with the white carpet in our house . . . She laid down the law and made sure that the kids knew they were not allowed in the "White Room."
>
> One day my wife was straightening up in that room, and she discovered a secret that someone had been keeping . . . a stain. She called me into the room and showed me the pink fingernail polish blotched on the white cushion.

We called our girls into the room . . . The interrogation was about to begin, but as I reached toward the cushion to expose the stain, my daughter Morgan cracked. She turned and ran up the stairs.

We eventually found her in her closet with her head buried in her knees. She let out the secret that she had been keeping for months. She had spilled the fingernail polish, and then she tried to clean it up. She scrubbed and scrubbed, but the stain just got worse.

She looked up at us with her big brown eyes full of tears and asked, "Do you still love me?"

My wife knelt down beside Morgan on the floor and whispered, *"Morgan, you could never make a big enough stain to keep me from loving you."*

Idleman continued, "Most of us are hiding some stains. Our worst fear is that someone will flip the cushion over and discover what we've tried to hide . . . because Jesus knows about our stains, we think that disqualifies us. Surely our stains get our names scratched off the invitation list to be a follower of Christ. He wouldn't want us. . . .

"The stain is still there . . . but a funny thing happened," he said. "Morgan started telling the story of the stained white couch . . . A stain that once represented shame and guilt and fear of rejection now represents love, grace and acceptance."[5]

Most of us are familiar with the Lord's Prayer. When Jesus' disciples said, "Lord, teach us to pray," Jesus responded, "In this manner . . . pray:

> "Our Father in heaven,
> Hallowed be Your name.
> Your kingdom come.
> Your will be done
> On earth as it is in heaven.
> Give us this day our daily bread.
> And forgive us our debts,
> As we forgive our debtors.
> And do not lead us into temptation,
> But deliver us from the evil one.
> For Yours is the kingdom and the power and
> the glory forever. Amen." (Matt. 6:9–13)

Most of us stop there, but what Jesus taught next radically shifts our prayer life. He said, "For if you forgive men their trespasses, your heavenly Father will also forgive you. But if you do not forgive men their trespasses, neither will your Father forgive your trespasses" (vv. 14–15).

Ouch! Being forgiven of our own sin hinges on our willingness to forgive others? Yes. Jesus said that God will not forgive us unless we forgive our children, husbands, families, and friends.

That's a tough pill to swallow. Holding a grudge can sometimes be a "guilty pleasure." Some aspect of our sinful flesh feels good when we turn a wrong over and over in our minds, thinking not-so-nice thoughts about the person who has hurt us. Forgive and let her "off the hook"? That wouldn't be fair!

No, it wouldn't. Aren't you glad God gives us grace, not fairness?

The apostle Peter once approached Jesus and asked Him, "Lord, how often shall my brother sin against me, and I forgive him? Up to seven times?"

Jesus answered, "I do not say to you, up to seven times, but up to seventy times seven" (Matt. 18:21–22). Now, my husband is the math whiz, but according to my calculations, that would be 490 times. Keep that number in mind today as you spend time with your children.

I pray that they will always perceive you as a mom of forgiveness and grace.

Today's Prayer

Today, say this special prayer of blessing aloud for your children. Read it to them at dinnertime, or go into their rooms and pray for each of them in person. You could also pray this blessing over them silently as they sleep. You may even want to type it up and print it out or post it in your children's rooms.

My child, I love you! You are exceptional. You are a gift and treasure from God. I thank God for permitting me to be your mother. I bless you with the healing of all wounds of rejection, neglect, and abuse that you have endured. I bless you with bubbling-over peace—the peace that only the Prince of Peace can give, a peace beyond comprehension. I bless your life with fruitfulness—good fruit, much fruit, and fruit that remains. I bless you with the spirit of sonship [or daughtership]. You are a son [or daughter] of the King of kings. You have a rich inheritance in the kingdom of God.

I bless you with success. You are the head and not the tail; you are above and not below. I bless you with health and strength of body, soul, and spirit. I bless you with overflowing successfulness, enabling you to be a blessing to others. I bless you with spiritual influence, for you are the light of the world and the salt of the earth. You are like a tree planted by rivers of water. You will thrive in all your ways.

I bless you with a depth of spiritual understanding and an intimate walk with your Lord. You will not stumble or falter, for God's Word will be a lamp to your feet and a light to your path. I bless you with pure, edifying, encouraging, and empowering relationships in life. You have favor with God and man. I bless you with abounding love and life. I bless you with power, love, and a sound mind. I bless you with wisdom and spiritual gifts from on high. You will minister God's comforting grace and anointing to others. You are blessed, my child! You are blessed with all spiritual blessings in Christ Jesus. Amen![6]

The Sword of the Spirit

For sin shall not have dominion over you, for you are not under law but under grace. (Rom. 6:14)

And He said to me, "My grace is sufficient for you, for My strength is made perfect in weakness." Therefore most gladly I will rather boast in my infirmities, that the power of Christ may rest upon me. (2 Cor. 12:9)

And God is able to make all grace abound toward you, that you, always having all sufficiency in all things, may have an abundance for every good work. (2 Cor. 9:8)

If we confess our sins, He is faithful and just to forgive us our sins and to cleanse us from all unrighteousness. (1 John 1:9)

And the Word became flesh, and dwelt among us, and we saw His glory, glory as of the only begotten from the Father, full of grace and truth . . . For of His fullness we have all received, and grace upon grace. (John 1:14, 16 NASB)

Small Group Discussion Questions

1. How does it affect you to know that God is a God of grace and forgiveness? How can you reflect His grace in your interactions with your children? In your prayers for them?

2. What concept did you have of the terms *grace* and *forgiveness* as you were growing up in your family? Has your understanding of these terms changed? If so, how?

3. Do you tend to be a forgiving person, or do you tend to hold grudges? Why do you think you are this way? What burdens do you need to hand over to God today? Release any grudges or unforgiveness to the Lord today. He says, "Vengeance is Mine, I will repay" (Heb. 10:30).

4. What causes you the most struggle in your efforts to offer grace to your kids? It could be a certain stressful time of day, a certain child who tries your patience, a particular habit of one child that drives you crazy, or something else. The next time this happens, how could you change your response to reflect God's grace and forgiveness? What words and actions might help change your child's behavior and attitude?

Epilogue

HENRI NOUWEN SAYS THAT WE ARE "A DIVINE CHOICE." You're God's choice, His beloved. So is each of your children. All of you are exquisitely crafted and passionately loved.

My prayer for you is that this book has touched your heart, stirred your feelings of gratitude, deepened your intimacy in prayer with God, and awakened your sleeping desire to pursue more of Him. If you've been hurting, I hope with all my heart that these words have been a salve for your wounded soul and that this book has inspired you to seek help and healing from our Great Physician.

I pray that you and your children have tasted the goodness of God, that you've embraced His will fully, that you've seen Him move in ways that have astounded you. As you have laid everything on the line in your pursuit of God, I know you've discovered that His blessings are new every morning; great is His faithfulness.

I trust that God will reward you for making it this far in

the journey, Prayer Warrior Mom. As you look back over the arc of your life from the moment you opened this book until now, I pray that you've seen increased fruitfulness, blessings beyond your wildest imagining. I pray that you've reaped a bountiful harvest as a result of your sacrificial prayers and your giving heart: that you've received from God's hand a "good measure, pressed down, shaken together, and running over" (Luke 6:38).

Please join in the spiritual conversation on my website at www.PrayerWarriorMom.com. You are a crucial part of our dialogue and fellowship together as Prayer Warrior Moms. You are a treasured prayer partner and sister in the faith. I can't wait to hear about your personal journey of faith as God has transformed you into a victorious Prayer Warrior Mom! Please share with me how the Lord has moved in your life and the lives of your children. Thank you for walking with me on this path to blessing.

Acknowledgments

ALL MY GRATITUDE FLOWS TO MY LORD AND SAVIOR, Jesus Christ. For who You are, all You've done, and all that You're going to do, I thank You. Your grace is sufficient for me!

Special thanks to my parents, Terry and Dorothy Martin and Jim and Joanna DeShong. Your love and prayers have transformed my life. I will be eternally grateful.

To my incredible brothers, Jay and Doug; and my sisters, Deborah, Colleen, and Cecilia, I appreciate your love and support. Woven through this book are memories of the fun times, the laughter, the tears, and the experiences we've shared. I love all of you so much.

To my loving, understanding, and supportive husband, you've been wonderful. Thanks for giving me the time and space to write this book. I pray that God will reward your sacrifices a millionfold!

To my darling children, Evan and Eden. Mommy loves you so much. Everything I do is for you. I pray every day for an outpouring of God's greatest blessings on your little lives, forever and ever, amen. May you always love Him, obey Him, and walk with Him.

To my agent, Mary Keeley, and the truly remarkable women at Books & Such Literary Agency. Thank you for your wisdom and guidance. Your knowledge of the Christian publishing industry is extraordinary. I'm so grateful for your help in taking this book from dream stage to finished product.

To my editors at Thomas Nelson, especially Kristen Parrish and Janene MacIvor, thank you for your encouragement, your skilled editing, and your powerful belief in the ministry of this book.

To my teachers, professors, friends, and all those who have inspired me, believed in me, and spoken truth into my life, thank you. You are a true blessing from God.

To the authors who have planted in me the love of books, a passion for learning, and a fiery devotion to the joy of writing—I will be eternally thankful. All those nights I spent reading on the landing of the stairs while everyone else in my family slept . . . in those moments, the world of books became real to me. More real than reality, even. And I thought, *Maybe, just maybe, someday I'll write my own book.*

Recommended Resources

Chapter 1: Cultivate an Attitude of Gratitude

DeMoss, Nancy Leigh. *Choosing Gratitude: Your Journey to Joy*. Chicago: Moody Publishers, 2011.

Niequist, Shauna. *Cold Tangerines: Celebrating the Extraordinary Nature of Everyday Life*. Grand Rapids: Zondervan, 2007.

Omartian, Stormie. *The Prayer That Changes Everything: The Hidden Power of Praising God*. Eugene, OR: Harvest House, 2005.

Vaughn, Ellen. *Radical Gratitude: Discovering Joy Through Everyday Thankfulness*. Grand Rapids: Zondervan, 2005.

Voskamp, Ann. *One Thousand Gifts: A Dare to Live Fully Right Where You Are*. Grand Rapids: Zondervan, 2010.

Chapter 2: Pray Scripture

Banks, James. *Prayers for Prodigals: 90 Days of Prayer for Your Child*. Grand Rapids: Discovery House, 2011.

Berndt, Jodie. *Praying the Scriptures for Your Children*. Grand Rapids: Zondervan, 2001.

_____. *Praying the Scriptures for Your Teenagers: Discover How to Pray God's Will for Their Lives*. Grand Rapids: Zondervan, 2007.

Moore, Beth. *Praying God's Word: Breaking Free from Spiritual Strongholds*. Repr. ed. Nashville: B&H, 2008.

Omartian, Stormie. *Praying the Bible into Your Life*. Eugene, OR: Harvest House, 2012.

Chapter 3: Stand in the Gap

Batterson, Mark. *The Circle Maker: Praying Circles Around Your Biggest Dreams and Greatest Fears*. Grand Rapids: Zondervan, 2011.

Dean, Jennifer Kennedy. *Live a Praying Life*. New and rev. anniv. ed. Birmingham: New Hope Publishers, 2010.

Ingram, Chip. *The Invisible War: What Every Believer Needs to Know About Satan, Demons, and Spiritual Warfare*. Repr. ed. Grand Rapids: Baker Books, 2008.

Sheets, Dutch. *Intercessory Prayer*. Ventura, CA: Regal Books, 2008.

Thompson, Janet. *Praying for Your Prodigal Daughter*. West Monroe, LA: Howard Books, 2008.

Chapter 4: *Satisfy the Conditions for Answered Prayer*

Heald, Cynthia. *Becoming a Woman of Prayer.* Colorado Springs: NavPress, 2005.

MacArthur, John. *Lord, Teach Me to Pray.* Nashville: Thomas Nelson, 2003.

Prince, Derek. *Secrets of a Prayer Warrior.* Grand Rapids: Chosen Books, Baker Publishing Group, 2009.

Chapter 5: *Pray with Power and Authority*

Alves, Elizabeth. *Becoming a Prayer Warrior.* Ventura, CA: Regal Books, 1998.

Cymbala, Jim. *Breakthrough Prayer: The Power of Connecting with the Heart of God.* Grand Rapids: Zondervan, 2003.

Delgado, Iris. *Satan, You Can't Have My Children.* Lake Mary, FL: Charisma House, 2011.

Fuller, Cheri. *When Mothers Pray: Bringing God's Power and Blessing to Your Children's Lives.* Sisters, OR: Multnomah, 2001.

Nichols, Fern. *When Moms Pray Together: True Stories of God's Power to Transform Your Child.* Carol Stream, IL: Tyndale House, 2009.

Sherrer, Quin. *A Woman's Guide to Spiritual Warfare.* Ventura, CA: Regal Books, 2010.

Tenney, Tommy. *How to Pray with Passion and Power.* Repr. ed. Grand Rapids: Revell, 2010.

Chapter 6: *Get Help When You Need It*

Websites for Women Facing Domestic Violence:

The National Coalition Against Domestic Violence, www.ncadv.org. For anonymous and confidential help 24/7, call 1-800-799-7233.

Focus Ministries, www.focusministries1.org (a support ministry founded by Brenda Branson, Christian domestic violence survivor)

Books:

Clark, Jerusha. *Living Beyond Postpartum Depression: Help and Hope for the Hurting Mom and Those Around Her.* Colorado Springs: NavPress, 2010.

Fortune, Marie. *Keeping the Faith: Guidance for Christian Women Facing Abuse.* San Francisco: HarperOne, 1995.

Johnson, Barbara. *When Your Child Breaks Your Heart: Help for Hurting Moms.* Grand Rapids: Revell, 2008.

McRoberts, Susan. *The Lifter of My Head: How God Sustained Me During Postpartum Depression.* Mustang, OK: Tate Publishing, 2007.

Nason-Clark, Nancy. *Refuge from Abuse: Healing and Hope for Abused Christian Women.* Downers Grove, IL: IVP Books, 2001.

Shields, Brooke. *Down Came the Rain: My Journey Through Postpartum Depression.* New York: Hyperion, 2006.

Stewart, Don. *Refuge: A Pathway Out of Domestic Violence and Abuse.* Birmingham: New Hope Publishers, 2004.

Zahn, Tina. *Why I Jumped: My True Story of Postpartum Depression, Dramatic Rescue & Return to Hope.* Grand Rapids: Revell, 2006.

Chapter 7: Learn to Love to Pray

Foster, Richard. *Prayer: Finding the Heart's True Home.* San Francisco: HarperOne, 1992.

Hybels, Bill. *Too Busy Not to Pray.* 20th anniv. ed. Downers Grove, IL: IVP Books, 2008.

Miller, Paul. *A Praying Life: Connecting with God in a Distracting World*. Colorado Springs: NavPress, 2009.

Patterson, Ben. *Deepening Your Conversation with God: Learning to Love to Pray*. Minneapolis: Bethany House, 2001.

Chapter 8: Be Persistent

Graham, Ruth Bell. *Prodigals and Those Who Love Them: Words of Encouragement for Those Who Wait*. Repr. ed. Grand Rapids: Baker Books, 2008.

Jacobs, Cindy. *The Power of Persistent Prayer*. Minneapolis: Bethany House, 2010.

Omartian, Stormie. *The Power of a Praying Woman*. Deluxe ed. Eugene, OR: Harvest House, 2007.

Sherrer, Quin. *Praying Prodigals Home: Taking Back What the Enemy Has Stolen*. Rev. ed. Ventura, CA: Regal Books, 2000.

Chapter 9: Fast for Spiritual Breakthrough

Colbert, Don. *Get Healthy Through Detox and Fasting: How to Revitalize Your Body in 28 Days*. Siloam, NC: Siloam Publishing, 2006.

Franklin, Jentezen. *The Fasting Edge*. Lake Mary, FL: Charisma House, 2011.

Gregory, Susan. *The Daniel Fast*. Carol Stream, IL: Tyndale House, 2010.

Nelson, Lisa. *A Woman's Guide to Fasting*. Minneapolis: Bethany House, 2011.

Towns, Elmer. *The Beginner's Guide to Fasting.* Ventura, CA: Regal Books, 2001.

_____. *Fasting for Spiritual Breakthrough: A Guide to Nine Biblical Fasts.* Ventura, CA: Regal Books, 1996.

Chapter 10: Hold Your Children Loosely

Bottke, Allison. *Setting Boundaries with Your Adult Children.* Eugene, OR: Harvest House, 2008.

Kent, Carol. *When I Lay My Isaac Down.* Colorado Springs: NavPress, 2004.

Omartian, Stormie. *The Power of Praying for Your Adult Children.* Eugene, OR: Harvest House, 2009.

Chapter 11: Hear God's Voice Above the Noise of Daily Life

Dean, Jennifer Kennedy. *Heart's Cry: Principles of Prayer.* Rev. ed. Birmingham: New Hope Publishers, 2007.

Jaynes, Sharon. *Becoming a Woman Who Listens to God.* Eugene, OR: Harvest House, 2012.

Shirer, Priscilla. *He Speaks to Me: Preparing to Hear the Voice of God.* Chicago: Moody Publishers, 2006.

Chapter 12: Be Your Children's Number One Advocate

Caruana, Vicki. *Stand Up for Your Kids Without Stepping on Toes.* Carol Stream, IL: Tyndale House, 2007.

Guarendi, Ray. *Discipline That Lasts a Lifetime: The Best Gift You Can Give Your Kids.* Ann Arbor: Servant Books, 2003.

Rigby, Jill. *Raising Respectful Children in a Disrespectful World*. West Monroe, LA: Howard Books, 2006.

Sherrer, Quin. *A Mother's Guide to Praying for Your Children*. Ventura, CA: Regal Books, 2010.

Chapter 13: Discern God's Will for Your Children

Eldredge, John. *Walking with God*. Nashville: Thomas Nelson, 2010.

Shirer, Priscilla. *Discerning the Voice of God*. New ed. Chicago: Moody Publishers, 2012.

Swindoll, Charles. *The Mystery of God's Will*. Nashville: Thomas Nelson, 2001.

Chapter 14: Live with a Spiritual Perspective

Burpo, Todd and Colton Burpo with Lynn Vincent. *Heaven Is for Real*. Repr. ed. Nashville: Thomas Nelson, 2011.

Chapman, Mary Beth with Ellen Vaughn. *Choosing to See*. Grand Rapids: Baker Publishing Group, 2010.

Dean, Jennifer Kennedy. *A Legacy of Prayer: A Spiritual Trust Fund for the Generations*. Birmingham: New Hope Publishers, 2002.

Chapter 15: Model Forgiveness and Grace

Barnhill, Julie. *Radical Forgiveness*. Carol Stream, IL: Tyndale House, 2004.

Fitzpatrick, Elyse. *Give Them Grace: Dazzling Your Kids with the Love of Jesus*. Wheaton, IL: Crossway Books, 2011.

Hunt, June. *How to Forgive . . . When You Don't Feel Like It.*
Eugene, OR: Harvest House, 2007.

Kimmel, Tim. *Grace-Based Parenting.* Nashville: Thomas
Nelson, 2005.

Smedes, Lewis. *Forgive & Forget: Healing the Hurts We Don't
Deserve.* 2nd ed. San Francisco: HarperOne, 2007.

Notes

Chapter 1: Cultivate an Attitude of Gratitude

1. http://www.brainyquote.com/quotes/keywords/gratitude.html.
2. Shauna Niequist, *Cold Tangerines: Celebrating the Extraordinary Nature of Everyday Life* (Grand Rapids: Zondervan, 2007), 194.

Chapter 2: Pray Scripture

1. John Quigley, as quoted by Jeanie Rose, "How to Pray Scripture," http://www.pray-the-scriptures.com /howtoprayscripture/howtoprayscripture.html.
2. James Banks, *Prayers for Prodigals: 90 Days of Prayer for Your Child* (Grand Rapids: Discovery House, 2011), 18.
3. Iris Delgado, *Satan, You Can't Have My Children* (Lake Mary, FL: Charisma House, 2011), 78, 114–15.

Chapter 3: Stand in the Gap

1. Jennifer Kennedy Dean, *Live a Praying Life,* new, rev. anniv. ed. (Birmingham: New Hope Publishers, 2010), 51–52. Diagram used with permission.
2. Dutch Sheets, *Intercessory Prayer,* Google e-books ed. (Ventura, CA: Regal Books, 2008), 97–99.
3. Mark Batterson, *The Circle Maker* (Grand Rapids: Zondervan, 2011), 21–23.
4. Carol Kent, *When I Lay My Isaac Down* (Colorado Springs: NavPress, 2004), 135–36.
5. Batterson, *The Circle Maker.*

Chapter 4: Satisfy the Conditions for Answered Prayer

1. http://www.christian-prayer-quotes.christian-attorney.net.
2 Joanna Weaver, *Having a Mary Heart in a Martha World* (Colorado Springs: WaterBrook Press, 2000), 17.
3. Derek Prince, *Secrets of a Prayer Warrior* (Grand Rapids: Baker Publishing Group, 2009), 27.
4. Max Lucado, "My Child Is in Danger," *MomSense,* July/August 2011, 16.

Chapter 5: Pray with Power and Authority

1. Leif Enger, *Peace Like a River* (New York: Grove Press, 2001), 4.
2. Corrie ten Boom, in Elizabeth Alves, *Becoming a Prayer Warrior* (Ventura, CA: Regal Books, 1998), 97.
3. *Nelson King James Version Bible Commentary* (Nashville: Thomas Nelson, 2005), 1579.
4. Jonathan Jordan, "Spiritual Power and Spiritual Authority," Thinking in Color, http://jonathanjordan.squarespace.com /studies-in-the-word/2007/6/23/spiritual-power-and -spiritual-authority.html.
5. Derek Prince, *War in Heaven: God's Epic Battle with Evil,* Google e-book ed. (Grand Rapids: Baker Publishing Group, 2003).

6. For a similar diagram, Elizabeth Alves, *Becoming a Prayer Warrior*, 126.

7. Batterson, *The Circle Maker*, 25.

8. Shawn Bean, "Are You a Hippo Mom?" *Parenting* magazine, February 2012, 11.

Chapter 6: Get Help When You Need It

1. Ann Voskamp, *One Thousand Gifts: A Dare to Live Fully Right Where You Are* (Grand Rapids: Zondervan, 2010), 26–27.

2. John Lennon, *Rolling Stone*, 1970, http://www.beatlesbible .com/songs/dont-let-me-down/.

3. Mary Beth Chapman with Ellen Vaughn, *Choosing to See* (Grand Rapids: Baker Publishing Group, 2010), 67.

4. Jane Rubietta, *Come Closer* (Colorado Springs: WaterBrook Press, 2007), 38–39.

5. Niequist, *Cold Tangerines*, 175–78.

Chapter 7: Learn to Love to Pray

1. E. M. Bounds, http://www.examiner.com /christian-living-in-nashville/inspirational-quotes-on-prayer.

2. Andrew Murray, http://www.goodreads.com/quotes /show/197572.

3. Voskamp, *One Thousand Gifts*, 35.

4. *The Strongest NASB Exhaustive Concordance*, s.v., "Meno" (Grand Rapids: Zondervan, 2004), 1546.

5. Charles Spurgeon, as quoted at http://www.examiner.com /christian-living-in-nashville/inspirational-quotes-on-prayer.

Chapter 8: Be Persistent

1. Dean, *Live a Praying Life*, 200.

2. Herbert Kaufman, as quoted at BrainyQuote.com; see http://www.brainyquote.com/quotes/keywords /persistence.html.

3. A. W. Tozer, as quoted at ThinkExist.com; see http://thinkexist.com/quotation/what-comes-into-our-minds-when-we-think-about-god/1211007.html.

4. Martin G. Collins, "Parable of the Persistent Friend," *Forerunner*, "Bible Study," August 2003, http://www.cgg.org/index.cfm/fuseaction/Library.sr/CT/BS/k/834/The-Parable-of-Persistent-Friend.htm.

5. Friedrich Nietzsche, *Beyond Good and Evil*, trans. Helen Zimmern (London: 1907), sec. 188.

Chapter 9: Fast for Spiritual Breakthrough

1. Quintus Tertullian, http://www.fasting.com/fastingquotes.html.

2. Jentezen Franklin, *Fasting* (Lake Mary, FL: Charisma House, 2008), 10.

3. Elmer Towns, *The Beginner's Guide to Fasting* (Ventura, CA: Regal Books, 2001), 109, 112.

4. John Chrysostom, http://www.fasting.com/fastingquotes.html.

5. Lisa Nelson, *A Woman's Guide to Fasting* (Minneapolis: Bethany House, 2011), 28.

6. Benedict Carey, "Parents Urged Again to Limit TV for Youngest," *New York Times*, October 18, 2011.

7. David Kinnaman, "The Mosaic Generation: The Mystifying New World of Youth Culture," *Enrichment Journal* online, http://enrichmentjournal.ag.org/200604/200604_028_MosaicGen.cfm.

Chapter 10: Hold Your Children Loosely

1. Robert Brault, http://www.goodreads.com/quotes/show/486386.

2. *Free Online Dictionary*, s.v., "Entrust," http://www.thefreedictionary.com/entrust.

3. John D. Rockefeller, as quoted by Randy Alcorn in *The Treasure Principle: Unlocking the Secret of Joyful Giving* (Colorado Springs: Multnomah, 2001), 17–18.

4. Amy Joy and Layne Olivo, *Fearfully and Wonderfully Made* (blog), http://olivo-fearfulandwonderful.blogspot.com. Used with permission.

Chapter 11: Hear God's Voice Above the Noise of Daily Life

1. Alves, *Becoming a Prayer Warrior*, 71. (See chap. 5, n. 2.)

2. Ibid., 74.

3. Stormie Omartian, *The Power of a Praying Parent*, in *The Power of Praying 3-in-1 Collection* (Eugene, OR: Harvest House Publishers), 87–89.

Chapter 12: Be Your Children's Number One Advocate

1. Marion C. Garretty, as quoted at the Quote Garden, http://www.quotegarden.com/mothers.html.

2. William Ross Wallace, from the poem "The Hand That Rocks the Cradle Is the Hand That Rules the World." Available to view at Poets' Corner, http://www.theotherpages.org/poems/wallace1.html.

3. Adapted from Tim Tebow, *Through My Eyes* (New York: HarperCollins, 2011), 3–4.

4. http://www.brainyquote.com/quotes/quotes/a/abrahamlin145909.html.

5. Mary Sheedy Kurcinka, *Raising Your Spirited Child* (New York: HarperCollins, 2006), 22–23.

6. Ibid., 28.

7. Ibid., 29–31.

8. For information on where to purchase the ChromaGen lenses, see the ChromaGen website at http://www.ireadbetternow.com.

9. Shelley Hawes Pate, "How Colored Lenses Help Dyslexia," *Dallas Child* magazine online, October 24, 2011, http://dallaschild.com/showarticle.asp?artid=1668.

Chapter 13: Discern God's Will for Your Children

1. Andrew Dhuse, http://www.quotegarden.com/god.html.
2. "Can you help me understand God's perfect will versus his permissive will?" Bible.Org, http://bible.org/question/can-you-help-me-understand-gods-perfect-will-versus-his-permissive-will.
3. Scott Adams, as quoted in Anna Muoio, "My Greatest Lesson: Unit of One," *Fast Company*, May 31, 1998, http://www.fastcompany.com/magazine/15/one.html.
4. David Sheff, *Beautiful Boy* (New York: Houghton Mifflin Harcourt, 2009), 173–76.

Chapter 14: Live with a Spiritual Perspective

1. http://www.goodreads.com/quotes/show/195520.
2. Chapman, *Choosing to See*, 141–44. (See chap. 6, n. 3.)
3. Ibid., 145–47.

Chapter 15: Model Forgiveness and Grace

1. http://thinkexist.com/quotations/forgiveness.
2. Philip Yancey, *What's So Amazing About Grace?* (Grand Rapids: Zondervan, 1997), 45.
3. http://www.quotationspage.com/quote/29593.html.
4. Angela Thomas, *52 Things Kids Need from a Mom* (Eugene, OR: Harvest House, 2011).
5. Kyle Idleman, *Not a Fan* (Grand Rapids: Zondervan, 2011), 117–19, 121.
6. Rebecca Greenwood, *Let Our Children Go* (Lake Mary, FL: Charisma House, 2011), 150–51.

About the Author

MARLA ALUPOAICEI HOLDS A BA IN ENGLISH AND COMmunications from Purdue University and a master of theology degree from Dallas Theological Seminary. An accomplished author, educator, and speaker, she serves with a variety of professional speaking and writing organizations, including the Advanced Writers and Speakers Association, Christian Women in Media, the Writer's View, MOPS (Mothers of Preschoolers), and more.

Marla loves teaching and ministering to women in many venues. She and her husband, David, operate a marriage ministry called Leap of Faith, allowing them to travel, speak, and mentor intercultural couples. Their website, Leap of Faith (www.marriageleap.com), enables them to minister to artists, writers, and intercultural couples across the globe. David and Marla are also active in ministry at their home church, First Baptist Church of Frisco, Texas.

Marla and her husband have a passion for social justice, and especially caring for orphans. They've traveled around the world, providing assistance and counseling to orphans as well as partnering with ministries such as Buckner Orphan Care International, Compassion International, Samaritan's Purse, Shoes for Orphan Souls, and more. Marla loves mentoring women and also writes for the website www.bible.org, on the women's *Tapestry* blog. She speaks on a wide variety of topics. To book Marla to speak at your church, women's group, or organization, please contact her at marla@marlaalupoaicei.com.

To connect with other Prayer Warrior Moms and to share your experience with this book, please visit Marla's website at: www.PrayerWarriorMom.com.